A Year's Exile. [A tale.]

George Bourne

A Year's Exile. [A tale.]
Bourne, George
British Library, Historical Print Editions
British Library
1898
230 p. ; 8°.
012623.g.37.

The BiblioLife Network

This project was made possible in part by the BiblioLife Network (BLN), a project aimed at addressing some of the huge challenges facing book preservationists around the world. The BLN includes libraries, library networks, archives, subject matter experts, online communities and library service providers. We believe every book ever published should be available as a high-quality print reproduction; printed on- demand anywhere in the world. This insures the ongoing accessibility of the content and helps generate sustainable revenue for the libraries and organizations that work to preserve these important materials.

The following book is in the "public domain" and represents an authentic reproduction of the text as printed by the original publisher. While we have attempted to accurately maintain the integrity of the original work, there are sometimes problems with the original book or micro-film from which the books were digitized. This can result in minor errors in reproduction. Possible imperfections include missing and blurred pages, poor pictures, markings and other reproduction issues beyond our control. Because this work is culturally important, we have made it available as part of our commitment to protecting, preserving, and promoting the world's literature.

GUIDE TO FOLD-OUTS, MAPS and OVERSIZED IMAGES

In an online database, page images do not need to conform to the size restrictions found in a printed book. When converting these images back into a printed bound book, the page sizes are standardized in ways that maintain the detail of the original. For large images, such as fold-out maps, the original page image is split into two or more pages.

Guidelines used to determine the split of oversize pages:

- Some images are split vertically; large images require vertical and horizontal splits.
- For horizontal splits, the content is split left to right.
- For vertical splits, the content is split from top to bottom.
- For both vertical and horizontal splits, the image is processed from top left to bottom right.

… A YEAR'S EXILE

A YEAR'S EXILE

BY

GEORGE BOURNE

JOHN LANE
THE BODLEY HEAD
LONDON AND NEW YORK
1898

Edinburgh : T. and A. Constable, Printers to Her Majesty

A YEAR'S EXILE

I

About ten o'clock one night, in the early part of a mild December, the opening of a front door in one of the more well-to-do side-streets of the Fulham Road contributed a much-needed touch of coloured light to the darkness which the few street lamps served chiefly to blacken gloomily, or dismally to curdle into the shapes of the small birch-trees, just discernible here and there against the sky.

A woman was holding the door open for two men to go out, of whom the first, as he passed, kissed her, saying, 'Don't wait up for me, dear. I shan't be back for a couple of hours.' He ran on down the steps, and opening the front gate, stood there in the light of the street lamp, which showed his own name —'Dr. W. Wright'—on a brass plate fastened to the gate-post, and exhibited the doctor himself as a man of average height, with an alert, clever-looking face, indicating a large reserve of chastened power in the man.

His companion, having taken leave of Mrs. Wright, joined him at the gate. He was a man of larger build than Wright, and, although as carefully dressed, gave an impression of having a fiercer strength of character than his friend, less polished and alert, but tamed by dreamy indolence.

They had hardly left their gate when, coming towards them from the other side of the lamp, a third man met them, and stopped. 'Why, Wright,' he said, 'where are you going?' At the same moment he and Wright's companion courteously lifted hats, eyeing one another with interest.

'We're going to catch a 'bus for Charing Cross,' answered Wright deliberately, 'and then across to Waterloo.'

'A 'bus!' . . . the newcomer began, in a tone of expostulation. But Wright cut him short: 'Yes; a 'bus. Mitchell, here, refuses to travel underground, and insists on going home to-night.'

'Oh!—this is Doctor Mitchell? That explains,' said the newcomer; and shaking his head with mock solemnity, 'We've heard of you. You countrymen, I fear, grow very prejudiced. . . . Think of preferring a tuppeny 'bus at this time o' night!'

Mitchell laughed gently: 'Possibly I've heard of you'; and Wright said quickly, 'Oh yes; this is Mr. Lane Thomson, Mitchell. And now come along, or you'll have to walk. You may's well see us as far as the 'bus, Thomson.'

Thomson, shrugging his square shoulders comically, began, 'My wife . . . but I'll chance it. For the word reminds me of *your* wife.' More seriously, he continued, 'You came to see Mrs. Wright, I suppose, Doctor Mitchell? What's your opinion?'

The answer came from Wright: 'No worse than I've all along hoped. Nerves a little out of order.

Only, as you know, I couldn't trust my own judgment in her case.'

Thomson chuckled. 'Yes, of course. You poison your other patients willingly enough, but . . . Well, Doctor Mitchell, and what's the remedy for Mrs. Wright? Change of air our friend here thought.'

'Change,' assented Mitchell, who was lighting a pipe; 'leave London for a while.'

A little plaintively, Wright began, 'I wish I could see how . . .' when Thomson interrupted, 'Well, there's your 'bus. You may discover a method on your way to Waterloo.'

He watched them mount to the top of the 'bus, noting how the London doctor buttoned up his coat collar, while Mitchell seemed to find his pipe sufficient protection against the raw night wind.

'A curious fellow,' commented Mitchell, as the 'bus rumbled away.

'I like him much. His wife's good, too. She and Emily are very dear friends.'

'He looks like an overgrown, red-faced boy. Did he ever need to shave in his life?'

'I doubt it. But he's a smart man. He's got an interest in a weekly paper; does the literary editing for it himself.'

'I suppose he lives near you?'

'That's his house—against the lamp where we met him.'

A long silence ensued. The 'bus was nearing Piccadilly Circus when at last Mitchell began, 'Why don't you get some one to exchange practices with you for a year?'

Wright assumed a look of amused forbearance

'You know half my practice doesn't pay,' he said dubiously.

'H'm! I s'pose not. . . . And for the same reason, you couldn't sell it?'

'No. And in fact, I don't want to. I feel that 'twould be rather mean to throw over so many people. . . .'

'I know,' Mitchell said. 'I've a kind of fatherly affection for the poor devils who can't pay me at home.'

For a minute or two he puffed vigorously at his pipe. Then, knocking the ashes from it on the side rail of the 'bus: 'Tell you what, old man. I don't need the money any more than you. You must exchange with me.'

But Wright sighed, and shook his head. 'You know you hate London,' he objected.

'Then I'll learn to like it. Besides, it's only a matter of personal taste—not worth thinking of beside your—beside Emily's health. If she isn't stronger by midsummer for her confinement, it may go hard with her; *you* know. So you'll have to agree.'

'It'd be splendid for me and Emily, of course,' Wright admitted; 'but . . . you see, it's different when you've a wife. I was frightfully lonely before I was married.'

'But surely—there'd be friends? Lane Thomson, for instance.'

'I know. But it's not the same thing,' persisted Wright.

Mitchell laughed. 'Of course not; or at any rate it oughtn't to be! But—hang it—who knows?—I might find a wife myself.'

Wright also laughed now, and said, 'Seriously, if that were certain, I'd consent at once. I can't help thinking of you as out of it—missing something, you know. A man . . .'

'Isn't complete until he's married? I know. . . . Well, then, you'd better let me shift from Rothwell for twelve months. . . . Not that I'm frantically eager for marriage. My work absorbs me. Only, at home I fancy it's quite as lonely as here. The parson's afraid of me: the squire hates me. He'd have liked to turn me out of the hunting-field t'other day. He couldn't, luckily for him, for he had a spill and broke his collar bone, which, like a Good Samaritan, I set for him. The other "society" so-called—well, I don't want any of it. So you see . . . ?'

Wright laughed. 'I know, but . . . ah, here we are.'

'I hadn't noticed,' the other remarked, standing up, and looking at his watch.

Nothing more was said until they had walked half-way across the foot-bridge at Charing Cross. Then Mitchell halted. 'We've loads of time,' he said, 'let's stay here a minute or two. This place always fascinates me.'

They leaned over to watch the river, coiling smoothly below them, and reflecting the lights from Waterloo Bridge. The clouds had partially cleared from the sky, showing one or two brilliant stars.

Presently Wright stirred. 'I suppose we must be moving along.'

Reluctantly Mitchell complied, and Wright said, 'It's very hard to realise that in a couple of hours you'll be fifty miles away from all this—and I at home. . . .'

'Oddly enough,' responded the other, 'I was for once finding it very easy. In fact, I had forgotten this bridge; I was on the hills—in the silence—at home at Rothwell.'

'I can't make it seem real at all,' said Wright, with a touch of sadness.

'No? . . . I had struck an angle with that star there, and reached home that way. A frightfully acute angle does it, and there you are.'

'Ah! . . . Just as I thought. You'd never be happy apart from those hills. You must give up the idea, old fellow.'

'On the contrary'; he paused, looking across at Waterloo Bridge; and then breaking off his sentence, said, 'Do you see the lights of the cabs going over there? . . . See that one going at such a pace! There's some one in a desperate hurry. A hansom, I'll be bound.'

'Well?'

'It's only a fancy. . . . I wouldn't speak of it to any one else.' He walked on, continuing, 'The people in them are just as real as you and me. Going on and on. . . . Think of their clothes—the men and women in those cabs and things—their hats, the rings on their hands, all familiar and *real* to them. . . . The idea's gone from me already. For a moment I had a glimpse of something— something in common with them—as if they and you and I were only a part of it. It's gone now. But I fancied that, if one could get his eye on that —that completeness as it seemed—don't you see?

I should feel as if I belonged to it wherever I was, and in fact be at home anywhere.'

They were just crossing the York Road. A pair of loud-laughing girls hustled past them as he finished speaking.

A sigh escaped Wright. 'There's your answer, I'm afraid.'

Mitchell set his teeth. Then, 'Why not? . . . Man alive! try and imagine it. When you think of me alive in the train presently, think of them just as much alive, somewhere. And all the people we've seen to-night. I want something to include all this, and wrap me in with it.'

Wright made no reply. As they paced up and down the platform of the almost deserted station, Mitchell returned to the practical question. 'I really rather like the notion of exchanging with you,' he said. And then, with a reluctant laugh, 'I'm half ashamed to confess it. But the unhappy truth is, that I've been getting bored at times. . . . Not often . . . still, it *has* happened. Sometimes I've wondered what it's all for—all this trouble we're taking. . . . You see? A change will really not be amiss for me.'

Wright saw the force of the argument, and finally gave a provisional assent to the proposal. If his wife was willing, he would take Mitchell's practice, for one year.

And Mrs. Wright consented gladly. A week later Mitchell was again in London, when it was arranged that on the last day of the year he should remove to their house, spending the day with them—a Sunday, as it conveniently chanced. The Wrights would proceed to Rothwell on the following Monday morning.

II

THERE is probably another reason besides that of convenience why the night rather than the day is chosen for friendly gatherings. Not only is it that daily cares are put away more wholly after the lamps are lit: in addition, the daylight is put away—the searching intrusive light that is not only yours and mine, but belongs just as much to the man in the street, and makes all the distance a partaker in our doings. But night brings with the need for society the means of having it undisturbed. It isolates from all but the chosen whom we would see; and so allows us to meet the more intimately. After nightfall along the street every ruddy square of light in the house windows marks where a drama is enacting, and, according to the sort of light, the drama may be fancied or, at any rate, the players imagined. And this suggests another advantage of the night-time; in the opportunity it affords, to one who cares to use it, of adapting his lights to the occasion or to the company, so as to bring out qualities into desired prominence.

Whether consciously or not, the Lane Thomsons took advantage of this opportunity so well, that the mere sight of their rooms was encouraging from the first moment of entering.

'I like *lamps*—so that you can shift them,' the husband would say in scorn of electricity as it had then developed, and in regardlessness of his wife's laughing explanation, 'You see, he doesn't have to see to keeping them clean.' She was willing enough that her husband should have all the credit for the artistic effect that the lamps produced. 'He always tells me that I don't understand such things,' she smiled; adding that she 'had never bought a lamp in her life'; whereat her guests marvelled at Lane Thomson's assiduity in purchasing, and took notice of his habit of springing up during his talk, to move a lamp into some more convenient place. Ladies remarked also that the labour of cleaning to which the wife alluded must often be considerable. Frequently at the Lane Thomsons' several lamps were burning where most people would be satisfied with one.

But, undeniably, the labour was not thrown away. At the Sunday evening supper-table (Sunday was Lane Thomson's favourite day for receiving guests) the brilliance was in itself inviting; and afterwards, when a move was made across the hall into the sitting-room, the change—cunningly devised, or a happy accident—was such as to put all into the mood for the conversation which was their host's chief relaxation. No one troubled to analyse how it was done; yet somehow instead of merely entering a well-lit room in which there was a good fire, all felt rather, throughout the room, as though the firelight itself had been *turned-on*, and was merely glowing here and there in greater intensity, brighter in some corner, or more flickeringly in the grate. If, then, one chanced to think of the night outside, the whole sitting-room was as a core of fire, in the thought, the mere colour of it aiding one to be warm. So again with the furniture, the pictures on the walls: everything was in excellent taste, well worth considering for its own sake, yet fitly subordinated; so that while nothing was obtrusive, all helped to put you into a pleasant humour for appreciating and being at ease with your fellows there.

These, and especially the master and mistress of the house, were the real centre of interest. Imagine in a darkened chamber a jar of gold-fish brilliantly lighted: from the darkness to the glass is a relief; the sparkling water is beautiful; but the moving fish there command the attention: and so at Lane Thomson's, all that you were consciously enjoying (much as the accessories helped) was the people you met. First, and if you were a stranger like Doctor Mitchell, you appreciated Lane Thomson even more than you did his wife. A big, ungainly man he was; whose bald head, at the supper-table, shone almost like one of his favourite lamps, and yet was as easily forgotten, for the broad, clean-shaven, rubicund face, alight with black eyes over a thin-lipped, appreciative smile. The smile became one of the unobserved influences of the room —always felt, even if unconsciously—when the man talked, in a voice which, at first hearing, startled as by an incongruity. How should such a big heavy man have so thin and soft a speech? Soon you would find that it had its charm, even as the thin lips had: that its undemonstrative, and almost caressing tones had a quality in keeping with the well-chosen words and the clean-cut vivid thought. Evidently it was not only in the matter of household furniture that Lane Thomson was tasteful, and knew what he was about; in fact, was it not over every other matter? His way of watching you as you spoke, with that smile of his warming you up and illumining what you had to say, while yet it always seemed to ask, 'Are you saying what you mean?' was that of a man not eager to talk; eager, rather, to listen; as though his guests and their conversation were a precious addition to the cosiness of the room. And yet occasionally he would talk fluently for the whole evening, if one were happy enough to wind him up to it; so that once, as Mitchell was leaving, after having hardly opened his lips, Mrs. Lane Thomson remarked demurely, 'Thanks for a pleasant evening. We haven't heard a great deal of you; but you have shown me that my husband isn't dumb. I had begun to fear it; for I have hardly heard his voice for a week.' That, however, was later, when Mitchell had become more intimate at the house.

Mrs. Lane Thomson's quality was less easily judged. What was she—a woman of forty, well preserved? That would have made her a more suitable match for her husband, who seemed to be at least forty-five. Or was she nearer thirty, but rather fatigued by being mated with one so much older? It was hard to say. Considerable beauty of person at least she had, perhaps never greater than now, and heightened by her manner of dress that winter. The black silk or velvet—she wore either on these Sunday evenings—flowing ungirdled in large folds from the shoulders, suited admirably her height and her restful movements. Its only decoration was a deep yoke of lace, which, opening narrowly, prolonged the curves of the throat and neck left bare. The same influence that the room itself had seemed personified in her: the dress-darkness wrapping-in warmly, the half-felt daintiness of the lace, and then the mellowed light faintly flushing on her face and glinting over the throat when she spoke. After all, was she not more the room's centre than even her husband? Did he not cunningly arrange the lights to suit her: match his voice to her character? She, certainly, provided a quality that toned together the varied elements of those Sunday gatherings, so that the predominating male minds lost some of their crude hardness and gained some sparkle. You felt that it was so, if for a minute she left the room, although you might not have been seeing or hearing her. The fire seemed to have blackened, until she reappeared.

But you could not analyse, or would not if you could, while you sat after supper round the fire, on those cold Sunday nights. The influences were too strong, and you could only feel comfortable and more alert for enjoyment of the time. Things ran so much in pairs, aiding one another's meaning, in that house; until the peace of adaptation, fitness, settled down upon all the guests. When pipes were lit, and the whisky was brought out, and talk grew close, then dusky fragrant thought floated about the room with the tobacco smoke, and quiet fun waited on the rims of the glasses. Sometimes a brilliant idea, or a clever saying, hung in the air all the evening, lighting all that was said afterwards; or sometimes a moment of close enthusiastic agreement between the friends was a presence in the room, an influence to be recognised and talked-up to, and that always somehow gathered itself like incense around Lane Thomson's wife. And yet the man himself could hardly take a second place. So massive in his person, so wide-reaching and with such a grip of things in his intellect; so readily sympathetic, too, in certain directions—he could, when he chose, get the best from his company, or wrap them round in enjoyment of his own qualities, like a soft-burning fire of cedar wood, with its pleasant odour.

III

HITHER, on that Sunday evening previous to their departure, the Wrights brought Doctor Mitchell, to introduce him to several friends specially invited by the Thomsons to come and bid Doctor Wright farewell.

Of these friends—excepting a Mr. Hartmann, who, as a lodger in the house, could hardly be counted as a guest, only one need be mentioned, an oldish man—near sixty, perhaps—by the name of Spencer. Mr. Spencer's coming deserves notice, if only as an act of moral courage; for the others present were well aware that he must have shown unwonted firmness, to overcome his wife's well-known objection to Sunday visiting. A hint of this to Mitchell caused him to look with interest upon the unobtrusive old man who was paying the Wrights so sincere a compliment. Yet there was little remarkable to observe about Mr. Spencer, unless it were the deference which Lane Thomson showed to his opinion, as to the opinion of a better-informed man. His manner of grey-headed kindliness, lit at times by a gentle humour, served well in giving balance and stability, where thought was apt to kindle into hot and sometimes heartless extravagance. In this, as in all ways, he formed a striking contrast with Hartmann.

No one regarded Hartmann's opinion in the least; but, on the other hand, his vivacity was liked by all, unless by Mrs. Lane Thomson, who laughingly snubbed him. He had the irreverence, and the enthusiasm, that belong to his age of five-and-twenty. Spencer teased him, and was teased by him in return; but those nearer his age—Thomson, Wright, and Mitchell when he knew him—took him more seriously; for his keen interest in what was new, to him, would for a time re-kindle in them the same interests, already lamentably dying down; or else it gave them the tickling pleasure of feeling that they were wiser than they once had been. Besides, Hartmann was acute of wit; almost unhealthily restless Mitchell fancied him, noting his paleness, accentuated by his dark hair and carefully trimmed beard and moustache. But then, it was a part of his cult to be very modern; his manner of dress proved it, no less than did his ideas. Many whims he had indulged at times, and had taken up with many a fashionable fad: Socialism, Theosophy, or now, under Lane Thomson's influence, the cult of Art,—no longer, during the winter, neglected for the joys of cycling. Means were not lacking for the indulgence of his whims. He held a good appointment in the Civil Service, where, as is well known, the salaries are in inverse ratio to the work that earns them. But 'they take it out of me in responsibility,' he said; and Lane Thomson admitted that, for a young man, it was a grave responsibility to handle an income so far beyond his needs and attended with so little constraint in the way of duty.

It was generally felt that evening that something not easy to replace would be lost when the Wrights left. About Doctor Wright there was a quality that made itself felt, although quite distinct from anything he said or did. He was a man to whom all liked to show their worthiest side, as if sure of its recognition from him; and was, in fact, one of the few men before whom other men dared show emotion. Mitchell knew that well, and was almost jealous when they returned home from the Thomsons', upon learning that others knew it also. He had said, 'Clever fellow is Lane Thomson, but the glitter of him is rather hard'; but Wright had answered, 'It's his manner only.... He came to me when his brother died; and then.... But he wouldn't like me to speak of it.' Mitchell's thought was, 'You see good in everybody'; but, had he been more watchful of the leave-taking between Wright and Lane Thomson, an expression in the latter's eyes might have struck him, and the memory of it might have saved him much subsequent trouble, when the expression no longer appeared. In fact, neither Lane Thomson nor any of his guests were at all disposed to be consoled by Mitchell's presence for their loss in Doctor Wright.

And Mrs. Wright? Without her, surely the rooms would sometimes grow airless, the conviviality rather dry and strained? To be where she was, was it not like being in cool April air, with billowy white clouds sailing through the blue? Beside her, Mrs. Lane Thomson's presence was as a clear and still September, golden and fruit coloured. Might it not become too sad, when all alone?

Still, it was Mrs. Thomson, rather than her guests, who would chiefly lose by Mrs. Wright's absence. Sitting side by side in the former's dressing-room that evening, their linked fingers had said much that the two women dreaded to begin speaking of. For some time they hovered round the subject, with many silences, and fitfully as the occasional flickering of the fire they were gazing at.

'Doctor Mitchell,' Mrs. Wright had said, 'has commended several old women in the village to my especial care.'

The other glancing quickly at her friend, laughed gently as though piqued. '"Old women" reminds me—Did I tell you how disagreeable old Mrs. Spencer was the other day? I had been saying how much I should miss you' (the other's fingers twitched upon hers at the word). 'She let it pass, looking like—like a village chapel; and presently began finding fault of some "new woman" whose friends were all men. I'm sure she was talking at me.' Again there was the piqued laugh, as she continued, 'Of course I agreed with her. I said, "Yes; we old women don't approve of the new. At any rate my husband's old woman doesn't." She shook her head, as if I ought not to talk so; but she made amends, paying you a compliment. In fact, she as good as held you and your husband up as an example to me.' . . . She sighed, then added, humorously, 'I didn't like to detract from your credit, by pointing out how it must be all pleasure living with your husband. . . . She would have thought me in love with him; and that would have clinched her case against me. Or she would have said, "Not with your irritable temper, my dear."'

With a sad smile and lifted brows she turned for the other's answer. It came, Mrs. Wright gently stroking her friend's hand while she spoke, still looking steadfastly at the fire: 'Why do you make yourself out to be so bad?'

'Because—because—Fred is really so good. It must be my fault. He is never worried by any one else. I envy the religious people. It must be so soothing to—to confess, and work things off one's mind. And to pray, too. I did, when I was little.'

'Willie thinks,' said Mrs. Wright, alluding to her husband, 'that the comfort of praying is easily explained by psychology. It helps you to get away—aloof—from distressing things. It makes them a little less personal to oneself.'

'Yes; but a woman doesn't want abstractions. *I* don't! I want *you*. To feel that you are near—it has been such a help to me—often when I have been cross. Even when I haven't come to grumble—and that has been often enough . . . I believe,' more gaily, 'I have made quite a drain-pipe of you, dear: and now—my dear drain-pipe is going to be taken away to the country.'

'But you'll be able to write.'

'As if I would *write* such disagreeable things to you! . . . No! what I want is to feel that some one is at hand who understands me, and will make allowances.'

'There will be Doctor Mitchell,' said Mrs. Wright.

'Another *man*?' she sighed comically, making her friend smile.

'He would understand,' Mrs. Wright protested.

'Yes, but . . . how could I explain about myself, without seeming to find fault with Fred? Poor old Fred! I want the doctor to love him—if only to help make up for myself.'

'But you do! But you do!' There were tears coming in Mrs. Wright's eyes.

'I do. . . . Only . . . but I am spoiling your last afternoon with my silly fancies. . . . Tell me about Doctor Mitchell. Fred likes him very much, but thinks he has grown slow and—mouldy, all alone in his village.'

'I know what you mean; but that will soon wear off. Besides, it doesn't matter: he's so *true*. And he *can* say the clever things that Fred likes. He made me think of you so vividly, after meeting you the other week.' She hesitated, as if appealing for approbation of this dear man-friend of hers. But as Mrs. Thomson waited, rocking her foot thoughtfully up and down, she continued, more hurriedly, 'He said that you had an *aquiline* tone of voice, very like your face in profile.' Watching for the effect upon her hearer, Mrs. Wright saw the other flush, not quite displeased, though saying hastily, 'What does he know of my face in profile? I don't think *that* at all clever. I don't believe it a bit.'

Now Mrs. Wright laughed pleasantly. 'It is proved by your tone then—quite aquiline. Rather proud and finely cut, with a lift of your chin. . . . Your profile? Oh, he's seen that photograph of you, and would like to have one. He admires it very much.'

'Oh, but . . . I don't encourage admirers with my photograph. That is for my friends.'

Mrs. Wright smiled. 'I told him that I would ask if you had one to spare.'

'Let him ask for himself. I should think he isn't shy. . . . Shall we go downstairs?'

Downstairs, Mitchell had already felt the attractive influence of Lane Thomson, whose tact was drawing him out, making him feel that he had some value, and giving him, in short, the comfortable sensation of having a place in the circle, and of being expected to do his part there.

IV

DOCTOR WRIGHT'S well-known friendship for Mitchell provided him with a circle of ready-made acquaintances, desirous of welcoming him to their houses. His slight lack of polish—at first amusing—rapidly came to be appreciated for its own sake. People liked to see his indolent disregard of tedious conventions; his rather curt speech, at times startling by its directness, had a savour of intimacy flattering to the hearer. And when, occasionally, he had given offence by looking unpardonably bored—he had been seen to yawn—amends were always made by the sudden lighting up of his eyes, announcing that he was about to talk. In talking, his voice became deeper and more rapid, his laugh fuller, while his hair roughened in a comical and quite unaccountable way.

After his lonely life, the abundance of conversation was a delight to him. He met many men prepared to discuss intelligently the ideas which he had half fancied that only Wright, in all the world besides himself, would be interested in. The men, on their part, observed that his views were practically the same as Wright's. It was left for Lane Thomson to point out that those views lost nothing by Mitchell's less usual way of expressing them—that they were plainly his own genuine manufacture, having the crispness of home-made bread. 'Mitchell has the more *colour*,' said Thomson; and the criticism was accepted. Where Wright was coolly decided, Mitchell was energetically warm; but he would often be indifferent about matters over which the other had been fastidiously sensitive. Women traced a resemblance between his manners and ideas, and his appearance of negligent strength. Watching his face, whose colour told of exposure to all kinds of weather, it was easier to understand and approve the differences between him and the pale city men whom he met. Women were, however, vaguely distressing to him. He was apt to feel shy in their presence, and liked better—in fact, could hardly have enough of—the unwonted touch of masculine intellects against his own. To say what he thought without fear of giving offence, and to hear other men doing the like in regard to all sorts of questions— this was for a time a veritable intellectual feast. And, good as were various others of his friends, nowhere could he enjoy this so much as at the Lane Thomsons', who had the additional advantage of being almost next-door neighbours to him. Several times a week he would call at their house, to enjoy a reasonable conversation with the master, or a racy argument with Hartmann.

On the other hand, with Mrs. Lane Thomson—the only lady with whom he grew at all intimate—his intercourse was confessedly not intellectual. As if by common consent, they avoided controversial subjects, preferring to exchange notes on matters of direct taste. And this was refreshing to both of them. After an evening spent in 'intellectual' friendship, a chat with Mrs. Thomson was to him as soft rain after sunshine, or as sunshine after days of cloud. For she was sunny, and again sad, by turns. And sometimes, during the first few weeks of strangeness, there would come upon the doctor a reaction from his new enthusiasm for society and smart talk: a desire for the faces of his old country-folk—shepherds, ploughmen, and women who worked on the land. He hungered to hear their slow thought, and to see them living in rugged patience through the tremendous frost that marked the two first months of the year. And he found that to Mrs. Thomson he could speak of them; of their patient endurance; their slow and almost stupid wit; their entire innocence of analytical thought, leaving almost naked in them the passions and emotions that grow obscured in more sophisticated life; and finding her keenly sympathetic, he secretly resolved to take her advice, and write about them.

Especially she was charmed by one of his fancies: that even during the severe frost, summer was present, or only a few miles up in the blue sky of those still days. It had receded, he said, but had not deserted them. Winter was but an icy wedge between summer and the earth; or, as she phrased it, delighting him, 'the sword in the bride-bed.' After all, what was summer? they asked. Merely a matter of vitality—more or less. He felt it still in his blood; she also, she confessed: and it gently mantled in her cheeks, to prove her word true. Meanwhile, elsewhere the vitality—the essential element of summer—was nowhere lost. There was the recent growth on trees: the colours burnt into their stems; the sweetness in stacked hay and heaped-up roots, all convertible into the fresh vitality of the cattle still extant on farms. She dwelt on the notion; and spoke of it again as 'your idea of eternal summer.' In short, whenever his new environment irked him, it was to Mrs. Lane Thomson that he turned instinctively, without at all knowing why. For indeed, what connection, what resemblance, could she have had, in her artificial and much polished life, with those men and women living in such nearness to nature that feature and skin, voice, and thought itself, seemed to belong to the ground they worked on, and to be toned and coloured by the weather that tyrannised over them? He neither knew nor cared to know, being satisfied to find in her the unknown quality for which he was famishing.

V

ONE night he had been to a concert with Lane Thomson and Hartmann, and, returning to have supper with them, was left for a few minutes with Mrs. Thomson. 'Why didn't you come?' he asked her.

She frowned hastily, saying—evidently desirous that no one else should hear—'I get so bored at these concerts. The players and singers are awfully clever, I know that. But so do they, and it *irritates* me so.' She seemed irritated at the very thought of it, yet gave him a sympathising look, as he rejoined, in the same confidential tone: 'To tell the truth, I was bored to-night. And those two have been talking of the "beautiful technique." . . . Well, I thought it *too* polished—nothing natural about it; a kind of bald head that one would like to crack.' He glanced at the piano, asking, 'Have you been singing? I fancy that would have suited me better.'

'I only sing to myself—to get me out of a bad temper.'

'When I'm cross I'll come and get you to sing to me.'

'It would only make you crosser. I can't sing. Fred laughs at the idea of my trying.'

'But if you like it . . .'

'I haven't time to practise, except when it would be a nuisance to . . . other people.'

Hartmann, entering, began pleasantly: 'Well, Mrs. Thomson, you ought to have come. . . . How nice your violets smell!'

She was wearing a small bunch at her waist; others were in water on the mantelpiece. She held the little jar to him. 'I'm glad you like them,' she said.

Mitchell drew in his breath. 'They make me impatient of London air.'

Thomson, who had come in, objected. 'They ought to make you contented, man! And there, as I live, are daffodils too! Now, what can you want of the country? I'm sure you couldn't get these flowers down there, in this frost.'

'What do I want of the country? ... Everything! I want a long drive between hedgerows to-night! Those daffodils don't appeal to me a bit. I only like the violets, because they make me think of the hillsides, where they'll be growing in another month's time.'

'But don't you,' the hostess asked reproachfully, 'really care for these lovely daffodils?' She was re-arranging them in the glass.

'Not a bit. They need the March winds and the clean air to make them precious to me. The violets suggest that, and I love them.'

'I see what you mean. But—oh no! I love them all.'

Lane Thomson, twinkling his eyes upon the doctor, while a smile on his broad face showed him ready to tease, hinted in his thin, fastidious way: 'I begin to suspect you of being sentimental, Mitchell. Confess you wanted a little more sentiment—soul, if you like—in the music and singing to-night?'

'I confess it,' the doctor laughed good-temperedly.

'And more of your old country-side Puritan feeling,' asked Hartmann, 'in the play last week?'

'Of course he did!' interrupted Thomson, although the doctor, with his glass at his lips, was shaking his head. 'It's all of a piece, you know. You never could have been an artist, Mitchell; you're too emotional. You should learn not to care, so that you may separate things. But you ask for morals with your comedy, soul with your singing, and March winds with your daffodils, and care for neither comedy nor singing nor daffodils for their own sake!'

'Quite true,' the doctor admitted, lazily helping himself to more wine.

'But don't you see the difference?' the other persisted. 'Now, as to these violets, I enjoy their sweet smell, apart from all associations. So I do the form and colour of the daffodils. So I do the qualities of a singer's voice, or the characterisation of a play. What *does* it matter, I ask, what *does* it matter, whether the singer is sincere or the play "moral"? I want to skim the beauty off from play, singing, flowers—to have the beauty alone for its own sake—to cut it off at the roots, and isolate it in a jar.'

'Yes,' the doctor rejoined ironically, 'that *is* art. Cut off at the roots from life, and with no hope of seeding.'

'I refuse to admit that,' Lane Thomson protested; while Hartmann laughed across the table to Mrs. Lane Thomson.

'I thought so to-night,' grumbled the doctor, 'when that girl was screeching. . . .'

'Hang it, man!' exclaimed Hartmann, 'she was singing exquisitely.'

Catching Mrs. Lane Thomson's amused glance, the doctor accepted the amendment: 'When that girl was singing exquisitely about shepherds and things.' He turned to Mrs. Thomson, and with an impatient gleam in his eyes went on, 'At home, an old man I know is minding sheep on the hillside by starlight—unless he's freezing to death at this moment. It's cold enough. The thought of him while that girl was singing exquisitely made me fairly ashamed to be there listening. I never heard anything more exquisitely false and dead in my life.'

'I'm sorry you went,' said Hartmann, in a mischievously soothing voice.

'So 'm I,' was the doctor's dogged rejoinder.

'But what would you have?' asked Thomson suavely.

'I don't know. . . . I think art should smell of nature, like these violets; not be cut off from it—divorced from life, as the daffodils are.'

Hartmann, looking keenly across the table at him, proposed that 'The question grows complex, if you apply it to the drama, for instance.'

Lane Thomson eagerly took up the suggestion. 'Ah, yes. Your theory will not hold there, Mitchell. Natural behaviour; natural morals—well, you know,' shrugging his shoulders, 'they are merely brutish. We couldn't have them on the stage, nor yet described in books.'

'Not the natural behaviour of civilised people?'

Lane Thomson smiled. 'The terms are contradictory.'

'Perhaps,' said Mitchell, as if puzzled. 'Yet, my old shepherd friend is very natural. But he's certainly no brute. He is, in fact, a very moral man.'

'Would he have liked that play last week?'

'I doubt it,' the doctor smiled dubiously.

'There you are! The emotional parts of the play —the love and anger—went as near to nature—brutal, savage nature—as we dare go on the stage. Objecting to it, a man would prove himself artificial.'

Here they rose and moved into the next room, where Mitchell began: 'It's a puzzling question. In morals I don't know right from wrong, nor yet always what I like. But in singing, though I can't tell good from bad, I *do* know what pleases me. Sooner than that girl who sang exquisitely—thanks for that term,

Hartmann!—I would hear a servant-girl singing over her work. The work makes it natural.'

Hartmann finished it for him sentimentally. 'Ah! the March air round the violets'; and laughed delightedly when Lane Thomson muttered, 'A damned east wind, I call it!'

His wife smiled to the doctor. '*I* have long left off singing over my work. But the servant *will* do it sometimes. The breeze comes from my husband.'

There was a moment's pause. A self-defensive, indrawing expression came over her husband's face. Then Hartmann rose. 'I'm going to bed'; and as he held his hand for saying good-night to Mrs. Thomson, he said pleasantly, 'You're tired, Mrs. Thomson. . . . I should send Mitchell home, if I were you.'

She refused his hand, and her eyes were angry as she said deliberately, 'I wish you would learn to let me defend myself. Good-night.' Then turning to Mitchell, who had risen, 'Sit down, doctor. I *am* tired, but I shall be vexed if *you* go before midnight.' Hartmann looked sheepish, but managed to say good-night to the others agreeably enough. And Mitchell, glancing at his watch, silently complied with the lady's caprice, although he fancied her husband uneasy.

But she sat down with a winning good temper that reassured them, laughingly exculpating herself. 'I have sent the servant to bed with a headache, or I should have gone myself for the same reason. But your talk, doctor, was almost curing it, when he must needs hint to you to go. Now, you'll stay till twelve?—that is only half an hour.' And then, suddenly turning to her husband, she asked him, 'You don't wish him to go, Fred?'

The animation returned to her husband's broad face as he exclaimed, 'Not I! I want to explain to him'; and he went on to explain his 'working philosophy,' heaping wantonly a strangely scornful pity upon Mitchell's 'shepherds and ploughboys and village washerwomen, clinging stupidly to a dull life which was a hardship to them, and no pleasure to any one else. My aim,' he added, 'is to have something to sting me into consciousness of beauty at every turn '—he glanced round the room—'and so I try to isolate the beauty—cut it off at the roots, if you like—so as to make it the more startling. Look—not pictures, but mere studies—hands, throats, bits of drapery, impressions of momentary colour. And in books the same sort of thing: isolated moments of passion, emotion, *cut out*, as you say, from the living people.'

Yet at Mitchell's smiling comment, 'A veritable butcher's shop, in fact!' he laughed. 'Bravo! for an instance, in talk, of the sort of thing I love—thought carved out and given in one tasty sentence. Why, it's *life*, my dear friend! Life itself . . . but as for the miserable routine of every-day duties, and care about our neighbours' doings—it doesn't deserve to be dignified with the name of life.'

But Mitchell refused to be serious. There followed quick repartee, with frequent laughter, in which the wife joined appreciatively, although she was very quiet. Only once she spoke, after Mitchell had said, 'I think you are playing with life. Still, I admit that it is a charming game you make of it.' Then she said pensively: 'Yes, Fred's theories would be delicious—if only . . .' and so, gazing at the fire, forgetful to finish, seemed to have travelled away into some world of her own, outside her husband's magic circle of art.

They were waiting for her to finish, hushed by her manner, when, somewhere out in the night, a clock struck twelve. Mitchell rose, and then Mrs. Thomson.

'Now, don't hurry away,' she said. Her husband joined her, persuading the doctor to stay, she insinuating, 'If you're afraid of tiring me, I will go on to bed and leave you; although,' she laughed gaily, 'I'm not a bit tired now.'

But the doctor was resolute. 'I must go. . . . I shall very likely be called up during the night.'

To her questioning glance he said simply—'A confinement.'

Her eyes flashed. 'How suddenly unreal you made Fred's theories sound!' she murmured.

Husband and wife stood in the passage, while the doctor put on his overcoat. With his hand on the front door latch: 'These pleasant evenings,' he said, 'make it good to be here. . . . But your violets made me really hungry.'

'Take these with you,' she said, as he opened the door. She took the bunch from her waist, placing them in his button-hole. 'They will revive in tepid water.'

'Thanks! . . . But don't stand here in the cold.'

Lane Thomson returned to his fire, but his wife stood watching Mitchell down the steps. She had felt him very sympathetic to-night. Yet as he looked back to her from the gate, the cold air at her throat, and the remembrance of what he had said about her profile to Mrs. Wright, struck at her at the same moment. Taking advantage of the noise made by closing and chaining the door, she sighed: 'I wish Emily were here!'

She wished for Emily Wright: and as the night wore on, the longing grew in intensity. The gloom of loneliness seemed to suffocate her: it was a black emptiness that no ordinary companionship could fill. Her longing was for a part in life where its pulses beat; she cared not about the skin of it at all; not at all for the vacant glittering or hum-drum affairs that filled her days. But the sweet, strong atmosphere of affection, strong and sweet as a summer night, so often inhaled when Mrs. Wright was by—this could sustain, if not satisfy her. How was it? The cold darkness became tremulous with the answer. Mrs. Wright was living for something vital: not only for her husband's housekeeping, but for his love as well. Yes; and yet more for the child she was to bear. See; in that she was one with all mothers; and Mrs. Thomson felt alone: apart from them all. She tried to imagine the countless women to become mothers while she lay there: and then her imagination focused itself upon the one—who was it?—then depending for her life on Doctor Mitchell's strong, sure aid. His too was a life worth living—how apart, in that, from her own!

VI

WHEN he came home to lunch the next day, Mitchell was nearly overwhelmed by the boisterous greetings of his shaggy, long-bodied little dog. Ringing for the housekeeper, he sat down and began to talk caressingly: 'Poor little Jack. Do you want to go out, then? Do you, eh? You don't like this nasty London: no garden; no hedgerows; no nice ratty haystacks, are there? Nothing any good for a sensible dog!'

The small body wriggled, and the short tail waggled delightedly. For this was a sensible and lovely conversation: and there was prospect of a run to follow it, with the world's sole hero and important person for a companion. Oh, this was splendid! Only—ah, bother! Mrs. Clarke is laying the cloth. And so, although it makes us stuffy and dull to be always by the fire, yet—it's nice too. . . . Ay; and they are talking good talk. Let the tail wag, and the eyes glisten up. Are they not talking of 'Jack,' and of taking him out? . . . But—pooh! now they are silly. Little dogs despise such nonsense; they prefer sleep.

Mrs. Clarke—old, skinny, and thin-haired—confesses that she *has* felt 'terrible home-sick to-day.' Her 'poor brother's son's wife' has written to her; and the old man 'have felt the cold sadly.' 'She says they all misses you, sir. No, he haven't had Doctor Wright. You see, none of 'em ain't earnt nothing this six weeks now. And my brother, he wouldn't like to ask him to call, same as if it'd bin you; not without he really wanted for something. Mrs. Wright —she called once. She said she'd come again and read to 'im. But they don't know whether she will care to; for they says she never goes to church.'

Mitchell, before he sat down, went into the next

room to change his coat. Returning, and stooping at the fire to warm his hands, his eyes fell upon the neglected violets, where Mrs. Lane Thomson had placed them last night. He took them out of the button-hole: 'Poor little things! No, not you, Jack,'—for Mrs. Clarke had gone, and the dog, looking up happily at his master's voice, sniffed towards the violets. 'You don't care for violets—one would think that I don't. . . . But we won't cremate them, old man! after they've been at a lady's waist.' They were tied with a narrow blue ribbon. 'How would you like a blue ribbon round your neck—eh, Jack? Not much? Not if it showed that some one cared for you? . . . No; they shan't be untied.' He stood up, wondering what to do with them. To burn them seemed sacrilegious. Mrs. Clarke was at the door. He turned to his writing-table, and dropped them into one of the small drawers at the side.

'Any one been in this morning, Mrs. Clarke?'

'Oh yes. I'd almost forgot. Mr. Thomson called. Mrs. Thomson isn't very well. He would like for you to go round and see her after you've had your lunch.'

'Oh! What's the matter?'

'He didn't say. But he said as he shouldn't be at home till evening. . . .' As she went out, Mitchell called her back.

'By the way, Mrs. Clarke, Mr. Hartmann will be here to supper to-night.'

He ate his lunch in a preoccupied way, wondering what could be the matter with Mrs. Lane Thomson, and remembering the slight friction he had witnessed on the previous night. Anxious for certainty, as he finished his meal, he pushed back his chair hastily. The dog rose yelping, and slunk, with drooping tail, beneath another chair. But the doctor called him out, sitting down penitently to administer the medicine of sympathy. 'Poor old chap! Did it pull his hair? And are all his nerves grown touchy with staying indoors so long?'

There was a tap at the door, and a familiar cool-sounding voice, 'May I come in?'

'Why, Mrs. Lane Thomson!' He hastened towards her with astonished welcome. She coloured a little, looking very handsome in her walking dress.

'Why!' he said gladly, 'I was just coming round to see you. They told me you were out of sorts?'

Again she flushed. 'Oh, it was nothing.' Her eyes, glancing half timidly at him, seemed to say, 'Don't ask about it.' She added, 'I had lunch early. I thought a walk would do me good, and I could call on my way to tell you that you needn't come.'

'It was too good of you to trouble,' he said. 'But I'm delighted that you were able to come.'

The dog had come to her for friendship. She was looking down into the pleading eyes, and smoothing the shaggy head. Mitchell watched her, puzzled. Did she wish him to understand something that she was unwilling to explain. Her manner had a curious air of embarrassment. Once before, in her own home, he had observed it; but to-day . . . He felt almost shy.

But suddenly she looked up, with a quiet laugh: 'I heard you talking, and was almost afraid to come in. I suppose it was to the dog?'

'Oh yes. Jack and I often have a talk.'

'Poor Jack! I hope he didn't mind being disturbed'; and, with a quick smile, as she glanced upwards to Jack's master, 'I heard something about "nerves." I hope it was nothing confidential?'

'Not just then. . . . Sometimes—' he laughed, remembering what might have been heard before lunch.

'Ah! . . . And are you a good dog, Jack . . . never repeating what you hear?'

Laughingly the doctor had begun to speak, before realising that his visitor's remark might be addressed covertly to himself. He was obliged to continue: 'I had put my chair back on his paw.'

'Oh, poor Jack! Was he cruel to you, old doggie?' The dog's eyes and tail responded to her flattering attentions. His master said, 'I think it hurt me more than it did him. . . . I have grown rather hardened to suffering humans. But in a dog:—I felt the twinge in his foot, and suddenly realised that he's a—a living thing—as much as I am. It almost made me sob. Poor Jack—this change from the country doesn't suit him. . . .'

Jack jumped into a chair to be nearer the kind eyes gazing into his. 'What a pity,' his new friend mused, still caressing him, 'that he can't know it is for a dear friend of ours that he is suffering! It might console him.'

'Yes,' assented Mitchell. 'Mrs. Wright's health for Jack's. We owe him something. . . . But he's ready to deteriorate, if only he's not separated from me.'

'You wise dog!' Her voice was very tender. 'You know what is better than health or self-development; something that makes it almost nice to have your toes trodden on, so that you may love. . . . I wish you could tell me all about it, Jack.' She stopped, with shining eyes that dared not look at Mitchell or away from the enraptured Jack. Mitchell, too, was strangely moved.

But his visitor stirred, as if going. 'Don't hurry!' he protested; but she stood up, and then, still loitering: 'Ah, there is Emily's—Mrs. Wright's—photograph . . .' she began, and then bethought herself that he had wished (though not to her) for one of her own. She added hurriedly, 'I miss her very much.'

But Mitchell was not thinking of photographs. He was speculating as to whether he could be brutal enough to challenge her to confess the real explanation of her visit. Merely to detain her, he said, 'By the way, you know that Hartmann is coming here to supper. Can't you and Fred come in too?'

She shook her head, a little sadly.

'It won't make any trouble,' he persisted.

'No. Thanks very much. Now that I'm well again, I shall have to—I mean, I shall go' (she blushed at her own correction) 'with Fred to the theatre. . . . And besides . . .'

'Well?'

'Never mind. I must go for my walk.'

'I was going out with Jack. If you'll wait, may we come with you as far as the end of the street?'

She sat down compliantly in the easy chair by the fire. Mitchell said, 'I shan't be a minute,' and went to the other room to make ready for his walk. The dog, all excitement, jumped again into the chair beside her for more caresses. He liked those eyes, and the soft touch of the gloves; still more he liked to be talked to. The low, kind voice could say pleasant things too. Its tone was answered by his affecting eyes; his thrilling body spoke in the same language as her caressing hand. In touch and kindly tone she was giving expression to the very thing that her words were trying to say, only too clumsily for his understanding: 'Poor, good dog! so you are quite sure that *you* love your master? And he doesn't call this little trembling body "hysterical"? What, Jack, eh? You are not merely soft eyes, and skin, and hair, and trembling flesh? . . . Ah! the tremble is what *love* is doing; and the hair and skin—are they what *life* is doing, eh, good dog?' He made a movement towards her shoulder and face. She put him back gently. 'No, no! They are only my skin and hair, my life, there. . . . You'll not find a tremble, old dog,—or not of your sort. Only hysterics. . . .' She was murmuring so low, that the doctor could not have heard it as he returned into the room; but seeing him, she laughed, with just a touch of colour: 'You say Jack is to be trusted?' and so stood up. Jack bounded from his chair, and raved about the room in frantic eagerness to be starting. But his place was coolly taken by his master, at a glance from whose eyes the visitor too sat down, wonderingly.

For full a minute, only the dog's impatient whining was heard; then Mitchell: 'You haven't told me what was the matter this morning?'

His look was distressingly searching. To meet it, she leaned back in her chair, with head thrown back, and so gazed straight at him. 'There was nothing,' she said coldly.

Still his eyes were on her; and she turned her head, looking, with heightened colour, at the fire, and waited until he asked quietly: 'Will your husband—will Fred—believe me, if I tell *him* that?'

Her sole reply was a half-contemptuous smile, that took possession of her lips only, and lay on them painfully. Her foot was moving uneasily up and down.

Suddenly he leaned forward, and took her hand. 'Allow me.'

She turned her head, with the repellent smile still on her lips; but held out the hand, noticing that his fingers were unsteady as he unbuttoned the glove and stripped it back from the white wrist. The contemptuous, self-defensive question was on her tongue: 'You—"hardened to humans"—cannot you feel a woman's pulse indifferently?' when he rose, and stood looking at the fire, breathing deeply. She suppressed her question, lifting her chin as she looked up to him, and merely asking, 'Well?'

He returned her gaze compassionately; in his turn asking, 'Well?'

She was very pale now, but she asked, 'What have you got to tell me? Something terrible?'

He sat down before answering, and then, sympathetically, 'My dear Mrs. Thomson, your *health* is good.... It must be you who have something to tell me? What is it?'

She turned her head to the fire again, quivering. Her treacherous pulse must have been talking to him, as the dog's trembling body had talked to her. Through a woman's wrist, might not the absence of love speak to an experienced touch, as well as its presence? What had this man understood?

He spoke again, with friendship in his tone. 'At least, tell me what I had better say to Fred?'

Did he suppose, then, that she wished him to lie to her husband? She smiled wearily. 'Of course you must tell the truth—that there is nothing the matter with me.'

'But that will imply that he was—mistaken, in supposing that you were unwell?'

Again her head was thrown back, and the half-contemptuous gaze was upon him. 'And that would be the truth,' she said deliberately.

'How so?' the doctor smiled.

'Because his intellect deceives him. He is so calm himself, so self-controlled, that he cannot understand'—she flushed, correcting herself—'I mean, that if one's mind is nervous—or ill-tempered' (she smiled deprecatingly)—'he persists in believing that the cause is purely physical.'

'Well, and what else is it?'

But her lips were parted. She was breathing hard, looking down and unable to answer.

Mitchell suggested persuasively, 'I think I shall tell him that you need rest—a change.'

She faltered, without looking up, 'But I don't *want* a change.'

'Why not? It would do you good.'

He took the hand again, and felt the excitement throbbing at her wrist. When he released it, she began to rebutton her glove nervously, saying, 'No; I don't need a change. I need to *be* changed, doctor.'

He sighed: 'Precisely the need that rest and a change of air would supply.'

She thought a moment; then, with her head still back, 'Please don't say so to Fred. He'll think that I've been . . .' She hesitated; and without completing her sentence, resumed despondently, 'And besides, he's always—it's always worse, when we are away from home.' She stood up, as though the matter were now decided.

'Ah, yes! when you get no quiet time at all. But I meant that you should go alone. . . . Have a fortnight with Mrs. Wright!'

For one moment she glanced yieldingly at the photograph on the mantelpiece. Then she looked down resolutely. 'No! I must think of Fred. He would be lost without me to brush his hat, and pour out his coffee, and so on.'

Mitchell persisted, 'It would do him good.'

Still looking down, but with a smile, she answered rapidly: 'Remember, you are prescribing for me, not for him. He would resent being done good to.'

'Not if it were for your sake,' he urged.

She felt unable to meet his sympathising look, until he added, 'And as for Hartmann, he could stay with me.'

With a glance of gratitude she turned from him, and taking in her hands the portrait of Mrs. Wright, gazed at it fondly, and so spoke, very quietly: 'It would be delicious; but—no, I mustn't do it. I must learn to be stronger in myself. . . .'

'My dear friend . . .' he began, when suddenly she threw herself into the chair again, and looking up pantingly, appealingly, cried—

'You don't know me yet! You don't know how weak and feeble and contemptible I am. I was disgusting this morning; I shan't be happy until I've told Mr. Hartmann that I'm ashamed of myself. . . . And I want to be good; but when I say anything to Fred, it vexes him, and he smiles and tells me not to be so emotional. . . . If he knew how cold and unfeeling I am! . . . And you prescribe "change." It is as absurd as Fred's talk. But none of you understand a woman. . . . All you care for is Art and Science, and Reason too! I go about my housework, hating the very name of Reason, and wondering what it has got to do with cooking and dusting and cleaning. . . . It ought not to be expected of us, any more than of your little dog. . . .'

Jack, who had lain down in despair near to the door, rose and came to her protestingly. The thick subdued passion left her voice, as she smoothed the dog's head. 'You poor little loving dog! I am spoiling your walk with my silliness. I'll go.'

'Jack,' said his master impressively, 'I can't submit to your dismissing my visitors, in the middle of an interesting discussion! Don't go,' he added quickly to his guest; 'I don't quite agree with you, as to the difference between men and women.'

She began again to make much of the dog, as a means of concealing her gratitude to the man for choosing to reply to her words merely, ignoring her emotion. And Mitchell, glad of her returning composure, continued: 'In my village, you know, the men are not artistic, nor reasonable. But there is the same difference. I should like you,' his eyes flashed laughing conviction, ' to see some of the old labourers and shepherds I know. Beside their stolid indifference, you would say that all these city men were a pack of emotional women. But the labourers' wives, sticking indoors half the year . . . well, I'll not disgust you by talking of them. It is a question of fresh air. . . . Not only for breathing, mind you. Those shepherds and farm-labourers live in the weather, until they are soaked through and through with it—skin and nerves and tissues—their very bones. I have set their bones. They sleep . . . and don't care a hang for anybody.'

Still caressing the dog, she said perversely: 'But we *want* to care! *I* do!' and her eyes challenged him.

He replied: 'And so you lie awake half the night, worrying.'

She forgot the dog, and leaned back in her chair defiantly, and interrupting him: 'Did my pulse tell you all this?'

'No, I've merely surmised it. I know I don't sleep so wholesomely here as I did at home. But I don't worry about it.'

She stood up, thinking for a few moments. Then, sadly, 'Life isn't the simple matter you think, doctor.'

He laughed. 'I know that, too. . . . If you're ready, we'll start.'

But she held out her hand, and with lifted chin and friendly eyes facing him, 'I want to be alone.' Jack leapt to her: 'No,' she laughed, 'have some fresh air with your master. *You* mustn't go having sleepless nights, you know.'

Mitchell laughed. 'Horrible to think of, isn't it?' She joined in his laugh, 'I at least don't *howl*! Good-bye.'

Late in the evening Mitchell was expecting Hartmann, when a note was brought to him from Mrs. Lane Thomson :—

'DEAR DOCTOR MITCHELL,—I shall tell Fred (I am just going to meet him and go to the theatre with him) that you say there is nothing the matter with me. That is true. I was only cross and rebellious this morning; and when I have told him I am sorry for that, there will be one confession off my mind.

'I am waiting now to beg Mr. Hartmann's pardon for something I said to him this morning. That will be confession number two.

'The third is to you. I am so ashamed of my behaviour this afternoon. I feel as though I had done nothing but complain of my good husband. Even if he deserved it, I should still have been very wrong to let you see me dissatisfied; and when I think of all his goodness and kindness, and how unworthy I am of him, I hate myself. If you had scolded me well this afternoon, it would have served me right; and I cannot tell you how grateful I am to you for being so kind and forbearing, although you must have seen what was wrong with me.

'I miss Mrs. Wright very much: but it is some compensation to know you. When I have her again, and you are gone back to Rothwell, you will have

the enclosed photograph to help you remember—
Your friend,   'ANNA LANE THOMSON.'

Mitchell looked at the photograph; then read the note again, and shook his head. 'She's trying to force herself to love him. . . . She'd far better go away for a week or two. Eh, Jack?' The dog, sleeping now before the fire, opened one contented eye, as if with a knowing wink, as his master went on. 'Wouldn't you be glad to see me again, old dog, after two or three weeks away?'

The letter and photograph were dropped provisionally into the drawer of the writing-table, along with the withered violets, and forgotten when Hartmann arrived.

VII

FOR two men of busy intellect, there are few games more fascinating than that of speculative talk. A game it is, deriving its fascination largely from the power men have (and they suppose it to be distinctively masculine) of 'talking in the air': that is to say, impersonally. Like a shuttlecock—or like several at once—the subject is bandied to and fro, wit following it quick as eyesight, and ready speech keeping it up; while there is but one rule to be observed—the rule that never must the shuttlecock be allowed to alight on either player's head. If this rule be adhered to, then there is no subject that may not be discussed, nor any thought that may not be expressed. A high adventurous life is that of the intellect thus set harmlessly free: flying easily and strongly over pleasant places, or fearlessly over the obscene or horrible. In fact, the talkers are like two magicians, who for mutual entertainment make, in the cloud of tobacco-smoke that perhaps hovers over their heads, a dim city which they people with images—imps, men, or angels—that talk and live their strange bloodless life, mean, brutal, splendid; while the two creators of them sit by to watch with interest, supposing themselves safe in their aloofness, and never attributing to one another any necessary resemblance to the anticking thought-people they are so busily creating.

By this sense of safety, and of logical irresponsibility, may be explained some of the occasional extravagance of the talk of Mitchell and Hartmann that evening over their supper, and afterwards by the fireside, with tobacco-smoke enfolding them, and glasses at their hand. Tacitly it was understood that they were merely at play together; and the game was so absorbing, that only at intervals were they conscious of themselves as something different from intellect, sitting apart from the play, yet—must it be admitted?—often more personally interested in it than either of them would have confessed, even to himself. Distinctively masculine, or shared by the feminine, this power of viewing life impersonally and in the abstract—of playing with a mimic world—is most blissfully effectual in concealing the too paralysing reality: the presence in the room and amidst all the magic, of the unknown living things called one's self and one's friend.

. . . . .

In the pride of this masculine power, Hartmann

and Mitchell were in the humour for pitying poor woman, who has it not. They agreed well in condemnation of emotion, with its erratic life—frenzied to-day, torpid to-morrow, and the next day replaced by emotion quite contradictory. A childish thing they called it: a thing that men, thanks to logic, may disregard. Hence they discerned two orders of truth: the masculine or logical, and the feminine or emotional. A very straw fire was the latter, burnt out as soon as kindled; but by the former, progress travelled its enlightened way. The two men smiled in their superiority, comparing Mrs. Thomson's penitence—of which Hartmann brought an account, with her husband's bland indifference, and applauding his 'pet paradox' that 'the art of living consists in hypocrisy.' Was not that, after all, more of a truism than a paradox? For if art consists in selection—in choice, then surely that, and that alone, is artistic action which is taken deliberately—not under impulse of feeling, but by logical recognition of what is most suitable for time and place. 'Hypocrisy,' Lane Thomson loved to call it; because often such action had beneath it no genuine truth of feeling, no emotional conviction, such as his wife, for an instance, demanded, but was much more a matter of pure play-acting; not unlike the cordial affection shown by women who detest one another, but play-acting better than that, and extended to all that one does. You might call it the new religion in fact, destined to hold society by the consistent bond of Logic, of Reason—mankind at last escaping the bondage of temperament and personality and recognising what was fit to do, as unerringly as painters recognise true form and colour, or as a musician knows true harmony. With men living thus, who would give or take offence? For when you have shaken off personality, and are dwelling aloof from feeling, in the calm realm of Reason, then criticism falls on that which you have done with; you accept with equal readiness blame and praise, seeing in both a contribution, an addition (as of fresh oxygen) to the white light of logic in which you live and move and have your being. A passionless Nirvana this, possible even on this plane of Being—if only, like Lane Thomson, men will live logically.

Truly it was a fine air-castle—this magic thought-edifice peopled with logical men, that was built by the two friendly magicians in their cloudy tobacco-smoke. Fine with the perfection of detail which generally, in such buildings, precedes their collapse. And the collapse came suddenly, without their well seeing how. Absorbed as they were in their game, and watching the bodiless, soulless thought-population of their cloud-town, they quite forgot themselves—the two strange living things for whom this evening's recreation was but a glimmer of their life—pulsing with unobserved appreciations and emotions. Had they remembered this pulsing, they would have seen it—even when they seemed most logical—shaking asunder the foundations of their beautiful City of Reason.

That they did not remember it was indeed strange. For surely two men who agreed so well in logic should not have differed—as all along the line they differed—whenever the applications of logic were made. There was this cloud-city, with its excellent logical laws—Lane Thomson ready to be crowned king of it, and Mrs. Lane Thomson, captive and quivering, dragged out into the logical streets for condemnation. And then, at every corner, Hartmann's thought-people, carrying the crown and the whip, were met and baffled by a mob of thoughts from Mitchell,—a mob sneering at the city's king and defending the helpless captive. How was this logically united city divided against itself—toppling to its fall?

Perhaps you may see how if, listening, you watch the two, and see their faces light up and darken, and their bodies gesturing with excitement, not over the game, but over the game's subject! Neglected emotion is there, pulsing through the self-forgetful magicians, and unconsciously swaying the crowds in their thought-streets.

For it is Hartmann himself who looks despondent, and not his thoughts (how can thought look so?) and it is the living man Mitchell who feels amused at the former's example of the paralysing embarrassment which feeling causes in its interference with logic. 'A woman believes only what she feels. And when Mrs. Thomson as good as told me this morning that my desire for the emancipation of women was mere humbug, why, hang it! I began to think so too. Some of her emotional scorn for me got into my own system, and for the time I had lost all my convictions. They were drowned in shame. In fact, I feel as if somewhere there is a weak place in my position, and that Mrs. Thomson has put her finger on it.'

Again, was it logic that prompted the subdued admiration in Mitchell's tone, replying, 'I have often noticed that quick insight — intuition — in women. They see at a glance what a man takes years to discover. Sometimes I think they must have got a sixth sense that we know nothing about.'

'Umph! I wouldn't change our power of thought for it; it's so uncomfortable. If it *can't* see at once, it only worries. Mrs. Thomson herself says, with her pleasant smile, "Women can't think; they can only worry."'

Surely it was not reasonable in Hartmann to begin impatiently, or to finish with a cynical laugh? Nor in his friend to flush with pleasure at thought of the lady's smile and speech? Hartmann, indeed, made amends with what seemed a profound observation: 'You see, feelings don't last; you can kill them by thinking, but you can't reproduce them that way. Perhaps the women can by worrying?'

Mitchell shook his head at that, and almost gasped at his sudden impulse to betray the secret that Mrs. Thomson, by ceaseless worrying, could not revive her affection for her husband. He spoke calmly, indeed, of his own powerlessness to recall certain vivid impressions, but all the time a warm, half-jealous gladness was upon him, with the feeling that not Hartmann, and probably none but himself, had been permitted by the distressed lady to infer so much about her.

And while they went on to talk of the uselessness of waiting until action is prompted by feeling — Hartmann referring, by way of illustration, to the small influence ever exercised by the Quakers' sect, waiting for the movement of the Spirit, and the doctor reminding him of a certain fineness about them when the said Spirit did chance to move—still, there was lingering about the latter a strange, unreasonable consciousness of something present in the room, not belonging to that talk-town of tobacco-smoke, but more alive than that—a feminine spirit, the equal of himself and his friend; as though Mrs. Lane Thomson's sixth sense had come in to watch their magic, or perhaps had lingered there since her visit that afternoon. He wondered how she would like some of their talk, and half wished Hartmann less violent in his logical scorn of the Quakers and all religious sects.

Then the city of logic began to dissolve away, as magic cities will do when blown upon.

For Hartmann was admiring Lane Thomson's 'hypocrisy.' 'It was really very charming, at times, to see how tenderly he behaved to his wife, considerate and indulgent as to a child.'

Yes; see the gentle art of living in practice. And then, observe how the barbarian natural man pounces on it to annihilate its beauty! For Mitchell, removing his pipe, spat viciously (perhaps his pipe was foul) into the fire, saying decidedly: 'The silly fool! She's no child!'

What! Anger in those decorous homes of thought? Hartmann, with mild heat defending Thomson, yet admitted that he might be playing the wrong part—a damning and ruinous admission, if either of them had observed it. Logic divided against itself. Mitchell did see it later—at night, and in bed—and rejected the art of 'hypocrisy' forthwith. But now he was listening, amused, to the other's theory of Mrs. Lane Thomson—a theory permissible (as all men will recognise) in the game they were playing: 'That, for any man less of a genius than Thomson (who had himself to develop), it would be worth living for merely to aid a woman like his wife to develop her own splendid powers. She was wasting now on stupid domesticity genius and emotions of the richest and finest order. Of course she grew irritable: he forgave her everything—every sarcasm even. She needed an outlet. The kindest thing, perhaps, would be to run away with her—take her abroad, wait on her, coddle her up, and see her spread out.'

It was said insincerely—a mere logical conclusion. Mitchell, not claiming a sixth sense, recognised his friend's *pose* of the modern man. And may not two talkers play securely with fire, such as this, in the abstract? He laughed. 'A very good move for an apostle of "hypocrisy."'

'No, no! Too decisive. For such strong action you must have some genuine *feeling*. In fact, be like a woman—as all men are when they are in love.'

'Ah! . . . I've never been in love.'

'Haven't you?' Hartmann sighed; and then, 'I have. . . . The girl died, though.'

In the silence that followed, their talk was quite forgotten. Again the feminine atmosphere seemed to invade the room—this time for both of them. Hartmann was dreaming of what might have been. Mitchell, dimly remembering several girls he had known, wondered at their lifelessness, their absence of colour, in comparison with the woman who had that day recognised him as a friend. And her friend he would be; would help her in her trouble; would keep her secret sacred—even from the two married lovers now in his own home at Rothwell.

Suddenly, with a jarring laugh, Hartmann broke the silence. 'We are getting sentimental—which is risky! Didn't you say you had been writing?'

Mitchell hauled out a short manuscript from his drawer, Hartmann having to move his chair a little out of the way. It was read carefully, and gently criticised; the final verdict being, 'On the whole, and but for those one or two faults, I like it. It's awfully good for a start. You'll do some more?'

Mitchell laughed. 'Yes; there's plenty more stuff. And I enjoy thinking about the country, now that I can't get out into it.'

The other, still holding the manuscript, mused a minute, and then: 'Have you shown this to Mrs. Thomson?'

Mitchell frowned and flushed. 'Nobody but you has seen it. You see, I admire Mrs. Thomson; but, after all, we're not much more than mere acquaintances. I've always fancied about her a "mustn't-let-him-presume" air.'

'Mere fancy. . . . She likes men, which is sensible on her part. . . .' He turned, saying, 'Shall I put this away?' and before Mitchell could interrupt him, he had pulled out the partly-opened drawer. . . .

Then, looking round with a comical smile, 'I see you've got your "mere acquaintance's" photograph here. And some faded violets, too!'

Mitchell lied, almost angrily: 'Oh, that was Mrs. Wright's doing.' He felt strangely jealous of this flippant intruder; who, moreover, would not leave the lady alone, but asked, with an incredulous smile still on his lips, 'By the way, she told me she had called on you. Did you diagnose at all?'

Mitchell bade himself be careful now; glad, too, to find that Hartmann did not seem to be in the secret. 'I don't think there's anything wrong. In fact, her physical health is splendid. I told her so, when I felt her pulse.'

The roguish, masculine smile returned to Hartmann's face, with his insinuating exclamation: 'Fortunate man.'

Mitchell flushed with sudden remembrance of the white wrist. But then, its owner's presence seemed to pervade the room; and he must defend her. 'Shut up, man!' he said; 'it doesn't suit you to talk like that.'

His guest's laugh was good-tempered enough: 'Why, doctor, have you got the woman's sixth sense, too? I could fancy Mrs. Thomson herself speaking then. . . . That sort of thing, pardon me, I despise. It is old, worn-out religion. . . . I believe in a man's letting his thoughts go absolutely free.'

'So do I—theoretically. . . . But then, hang it!' —he looked puzzled—'why not his feelings, too?'

Why not? Why not anything in the game of conversation? Straightway they fell to building in the air again. But now, although Art and Logic were not excluded from the new dim streets, it was rather as serene ideals—the statues in the public places—that these reappeared than as living denizens of the republic. Perhaps because Mitchell was the more ardent of the two in talking, and smoked the more fiercely, the world they contemplated in the midnight hours (always above their heads—oh, of course!) was peopled less with images of Lane Thomson than with a folk drifting aimlessly—tumultuous with passions, with neither king to rule, nor law to guide. A folk obeying always their impulses —because, as it was said (and the saying was surely characteristic of the man of science), 'we don't know right from wrong, good from bad: only results can prove. There is no law but that of natural selection. Let every man develop himself to the utmost—*all* of himself—and every woman too' (remember that we are talking 'in the air'). 'Good and bad alike, let them all have way; for the fiercer the struggle, the finer and more advanced will be the types surviving from it.'

Hartmann's contributions were cynical; for Mitchell having remarked, 'There's never any reason to fear evil; the bad *can't* last. Only the fit to survive can survive,' Hartmann queried pathetically, 'And if you're a wrong 'un yourself?'

'Why—then you're snuffed out,—or your children are. But you've tried another experiment for the race.'

'Ah! very self-denying. Like the man in doubt as to whether it was a mushroom or a toadstool that he had found.'

Mitchell laughed; but insisted, 'You can't think how tolerant this makes me feel towards all sorts of errors.'

And so, having discarded current codes and systems, and in faith for the future, they left their chaotic republic without guidance, except that of the strongest impulse of the moment. And mayhap that is guide good enough, in the world of tobacco-smoke, and for the sprites that dwell there: whether good enough for two men with their strongest impulses sometimes coming into conflict, is another question.

VIII

BETWEEN Mitchell and his old housekeeper, Mrs. Clarke, there existed mutual regard amounting, on her side, to deep-felt though silent affection. Long ago she had been a valued servant in Mitchell's family; she had cared for him when his mother died, and had, in fact, deferred her marriage until he was old enough to be sent to school. The years of trouble that followed for her, leaving her alone in the world, except for her now helpless old brother at Rothwell, and practically without means too, had not cooled her almost motherly tenderness for her 'young Mr. Charlie.' And yet she took such pride in serving him, in 'knowing her place,' and behaving with the old-fashioned respect which seemed his due, that Mitchell was hardly aware of more in her than gratitude to him for saving her from destitution. So, too, on her part, she little suspected how much he appreciated her, or how he felt himself still under an almost sacred obligation to care for her in return for her long past care for him. At first, when she became his housekeeper, it had distressed her that he seemed to have lost the religion she had tried to implant in him; but long ago she had found comfort in reflecting that he was a true Christian in deed, if not in word. And perhaps this explanation of his unfailing courtesy to her pleased her better than the truer and more flattering one could have done; for she had no idea of that strong personal liking of his for straightforward and simple-hearted folk, which had made him the friend of the villagers at Rothwell. Their opinion was hers also, that in the main, and in spite of his being a 'scholard' and a 'gentleman,' his interests were the same as theirs.

But when, realising how dull she must find it in London, away from all her acquaintances, he passed on to her the journals and magazines he bought, an ill-defined uneasiness began to take hold of her. He had told her of the theatres he visited; and he bought one or two portraits of the actresses who played there. There were occasionally pictures that startled her in the books; and as she read the letter-press she wondered, with ever-growing pain, why he should buy such books as these. They ought never to be allowed, she thought.

Properly, of course, she belonged to those earlier generations that just sufficed to keep the country alive until our own time; and to her the Future of the Drama, the Illustration of Books, the Problem Novel, and other such momentous matters were of paramount unimportance. One sense alone had been cultivated in her, with the narrow academic culture of the State Establishment; and this sense, thanks to the journals she read, was quickened into painful suspicion of the new influences surrounding her beloved master.

At first the suspicion was vague; an unformulated dread: or, at the most, formulated only as a hope that his pleasant temper would not lead him into bad society. Of all his friends she felt doubtful; the more easily, because she knew nothing about them; and little by little, as if by instinct, she became especially dubious over his growing familiarity with the Lane Thomsons. There may have been some feeling of jealousy too when she shook her grey head, murmuring to herself that 'new brooms sweep clean; but old friends are the best in the long-run.' She wished he wasn't 'so thick with folks he hadn't known six weeks.'

At length—it was misery to her—her alarms began to take shape. Mrs. Lane Thomson's pretty housemaid—a girl from Rothwell, whom Mrs. Clarke herself had recommended, had been gossiping with Mitchell's servant, who brought home to the housekeeper a somewhat astonished account of the lady's animated spirits, after her visit to Doctor Mitchell. Such talk was severely rebuked by Mrs. Clarke; and two days later the girl was threatened with dismissal for spying. Entering the doctor's room, when she supposed him out, she had, she said, seen him replace something in a drawer of his writing-table; and later, when dusting the room, had observed in that same drawer a portrait of Mrs. Lane Thomson, and no other! After that, Mrs. Clarke took care always to dust the room herself; hurrying past the suspected drawers, lest she should be tempted to peep and find—what she dared not see. How, without overstepping the bounds of a dependant's respect, to warn her innocent young master of the wiles of womankind, was a problem she could nowise solve.

Once, indeed, she made a timid attempt. He went again, with the Lane Thomsons of course, to a theatre: and Mrs. Clarke ventured a hope that it wasn't like some of those she had read about, that didn't seem to be any better than they should be. He realised that she disapproved of the modern drama. 'It seems all against English feeling,' she said, solemnly. His own tolerance of it was so obvious that to object further was to criticise him,—a thing incompatible with her duty. She gave up the attempt for that time.

At Lane Thomson's the doctor idly repeated what she had said. With his most exquisite smile Thomson admitted: 'Yes; it *is* against English feeling. We've no national feeling for Art in any of its forms.'

The wife's comment was surprising: 'I don't know. We've a national feeling for the art of morals.'

Her husband laughed. 'Mrs. Grundy as an artist —a good idea for an article, Nan.'

Mrs. Thomson observed carelessly, 'You're not capable of treating it'; and turned to Mitchell, saying that she should like to know Mrs. Clarke better.

The doctor seized gladly upon the idea. 'It would be a real kindness if you would ask her to tea with you somewhere. She's lonely here.'

He was commissioned to invite Mrs. Clarke for the following afternoon. The housekeeper was urged to go because 'it would do Mrs. Thomson good. She's lonely'—a suggestion that spoilt Mrs. Clarke's pleasure in the anticipation of her visit. But it was of herself alone that she asked the question: 'How should *he* know she's lonely?' and only to herself that it was said: 'She has company enough, though she may make out not, to him.' And then inconsistently the simple old lady brooded over the thought of the influence a lonely-feeling woman might exercise upon a warm-hearted young man. Mitchell's thirty-five years seemed to her a dangerously youthful age.

She returned from her visit with an easier mind. Mrs. Lane Thomson's kitchen, very still and cosy in the raw, winter afternoon, and the pleasant sitting-room with its bright fire and tidy hearth, had spoken to her, in a language she could understand, of orderly life. The servant was out, and they had washed their own tea-things together; Mrs. Clarke silently watching the lady's practised hands—not too good, it appeared, to be useful, for all their delicacy. And then by the fireside they had talked for an hour. Or—who had talked? Herself, chiefly; for she had taken no work, and had been almost forced to sit in unaccustomed idleness, wondering more and more to see her hostess lighting the lamp, putting on coals, and at last settling down calmly to some plain needlework, as though she thought herself no better than ordinary women. 'I want you to be idle for a whole hour, Mrs. Clarke, and tell me about your home at Rothwell. I should so like to see it.' Accordingly Mrs. Clarke had told, stimulated by glances of smiling appreciation from womanly eyes lifted momentarily over the needlework. And once, when the tale was of the housekeeper's old, worn-out brother, suffering during the terrible winter, although not in actual want—'for I sends him some, and so does Doctor Mitchell'—the needlework was forgotten, while over parted lips Mrs. Thomson's eyes glistened sympathy that won the old lady's heart for a time.

But at night, thought returned, and the devil of suspicion with it, as though he and thought were inseparables. She was telling of her pleasant afternoon to the doctor, late home and tired with influenza cases. A niece, she had been asked to say, was shortly coming to live at Mr. Thomson's; 'a young lady wanting to study music at some place in London.' Why should her master's tired face light up, and he exclaim: 'Ah! then perhaps Mrs. Thomson will be able to get a holiday. I want her to go down to Rothwell for a week or two?'

Now, why should he? And why had Mrs. Thomson been eager for the same thing? And listen: 'I hope you've done her as much good as she seems to have done you, Mrs. Clarke.'

'She didn't seem to me to be in want of doing good, sir.'

Could it be, then, that her alleged dulness had been invented by her as an excuse for inviting the old housekeeper, in order to 'get round her' somehow? Well, then, the housekeeper would not go next week, as she had been asked. She wasn't one to be taken-in twice by a handsome face: not like a poor innocent young man. . . .

But suspicion is a cruel and hard-driving fiend. When the time came, Mrs. Clarke was unable to keep away. 'If I get half a chance, when she seems so cheerful, I'll tax her with pretending to be dull.'

It chanced, however, that on this occasion Mrs. Thomson appeared to be undoubtedly in low spirits. Yet there was still about her that friendly charm which thought with its accompanying devil had forgotten, but which appealed again to Mrs. Clarke's sympathies; and instead of the intended expostulation, she made, ere she left, quite a different kind of appeal.

The cause of the lady's melancholy was slow to appear; for, much as she felt drawn to her aged guest, her quicker wit could not easily accommodate itself to the other's simplicity. Besides, their language was different, not so much in words, as in weight. Although she could not have explained it, Mrs. Thomson was acutely conscious of that, and feared to express half her meaning, because she could not allow for the inevitable magnifying of it in her guest's understanding.

Mitchell had warned her of this. 'The few words they possess have to be loaded up with all sorts of meaning that we shouldn't put on their backs.'

'Like overburdened asses,' Lane Thomson had suggested.

'Or like a shilling that has to go a long way where shillings are scarce,' the doctor had replied.

Remembering this, Mrs. Lane Thomson was prepared for something forcible, laconic. But the force she found was of another kind, which puzzled and constrained, while at the same time it attracted her. Except for a simple kind of dignity, Mrs. Clarke had neither force nor wit. Her mind seemed tremulous and shrunken as her hands; there was no stamp of originality about what she said; in fact, it had all the impersonality of platitude. Old-fashioned platitude; the traditional opinion of the folk, sometimes bordering on the proverbial: that was the characteristic of Mrs. Clarke's talk. It said not what she thought and felt, so much as what her class had thought and felt, scattered about in semi-silence all over England, for centuries; and perhaps this it was that gave the impression of weighty truth to simplest sayings.

'I wanted to talk to you about Fanny,' Mrs. Thomson began, alluding to her housemaid. 'Do you know she's got a sweetheart?'

'Not in London, I hope, ma'am? There was a young man keepin' company with her before she came here.'

'That's what I mean.... But do they really think seriously of being married?'..

'You don't know no reason for why not, do you, ma'am?' The old housekeeper spoke apprehensively.

'She's not twenty yet,' objected Mrs. Thomson, steadily darning away at one of her husband's socks. 'If she marries so young, she'll have a big family and be an old woman before she's thirty. And she's so pretty now; it seems a shame to think of spoiling such a bright, happy-looking life.'

'Well, of course there is that way of looking at it. But it's best for 'em to have their troubles while they're young and can work. They've got to go through it somewhen.'

'Ah—that's it. *Have* they got to go through it? Wouldn't it be wiser to wait?'

'Why should they? I like to see 'em marry while they loves one another, and are ready to put up with a little hardship for the sake of it.' The old lady went on vigorously with her sewing.

'But—they get such large families.... It makes them so poor.'

The old lady sighed, but said, 'It don't hurt 'em though, to have to work hard.'

'Ah—but the poor little children, Mrs. Clarke.

How can they be properly cared for? They have no chance to be anything better than their father and mother.'

Mrs. Clarke shook her head. 'I don't see what for they should want to be. There's too many of 'em as it is wanting to get up above their station. My poor brother have often said all they learn in school is to be afraid of hard work.'

Mrs. Thomson stared. 'But surely . . . what is good for their . . . for us, is good for them? Why shouldn't they learn to enjoy pleasant things—as Doctor Mitchell does, for instance?'

At this reminder of her master's suspected pleasures, Mrs. Clarke grew dogged. 'I don't see that he's any the better for it,' she said. 'Somebody's got to do the work. We can't live by going to the theatre and—and—amusing ourselves, ma'am. Your Fanny wouldn't be none the better woman for playing the piano instead of having a family of children to do for.'

It was tantamount to a criticism on Mrs. Thomson's own life. Resentfully she broke off a fresh piece of worsted, and, threading her needle, said with a touch of heat: 'I can't see that she'd be any the better for having a family and no means to bring them up.'

'He's a steady chap, is her sweetheart, and 'll make her a good husband, I'll be bound.'

'I'm glad to hear you say so,' replied the lady impatiently, slowly forgetting the difference between them. 'But,' she continued, 'Mrs. Wright tells me that he's only earning eighteen shillings a week. It seems to me positively wicked to think of taking a poor girl from a comfortable home. . . .'

Mrs. Clarke laughed. 'She's one of eight that was bred up on less than that.'

What could Mrs. Thomson say? These folk seemed to care nothing for the delights of art and a cultured life. And as for robust physical well-being —it was demonstrated possible, by Fanny's own rustic comeliness.

Mrs. Clarke added: 'Her parents was married young, and lived and worked hard. But it hasn't hurt 'em, you see.'

Obviously not; if the children were content to be ploughboys and servants, not going to the theatre or playing the piano. Mrs. Thomson was baffled; and rather scornfully she said, 'I see you don't believe in over-population, Mrs. Clarke. . . . I fancy Doctor Mitchell does, though, from something he said the other night about these crowded London places.'

'I don't know what he says. . . . But why does he go out, at all times o' the night, to childbirths, if he don't believe in it?'

Mrs. Thomson put down her hands into her lap, and gazed at her visitor, her lips parted. Then, seeing that the fire was getting low, she knelt down on the hearth to attend to it; and her mind went back to that sleepless night she had passed, in thinking over this very subject.

The room was very still; and the flame that sprang up in the fire showed, by its red, darting reflection from the furniture, how the afternoon was already darkening. It was one of those moments when new unthought-of ideas present themselves to the mind; and Mrs. Thomson, as she knelt there, looked dreamily into the fire, wondering what could be that feeling that constrained Mitchell against his opinions, and that seemed to have saturated Mrs. Clarke and all her uncultured class. . . . A feeling for the continuity of life. Had she got it, herself? And if so, what was her life worth—childless? . . .

Mrs. Clarke, who had not spoken, began to fold up her work. 'It's getting dark; and I must be going,' she said.

The other, without rising, put her hand on to the old woman's knees, as though to keep her still. 'Don't hurry,' she said. 'I was thinking . . . perhaps I've no right to have an opinion on—on what we've been talking of. . . . I'm rather envious of Mrs. Wright. I want some one to love;—a little one of my own.'

Instinctively—it was a mother's action—the elder woman put down her own hand upon the hand that touched her. 'You're spared a great deal, Mrs. Thomson.'

'Ah! but—isn't it better for a woman to have to bear it. Before you came, I'd been feeling so: and now your talk has made me . . . I feel ashamed—as if I'm different—cut off from all the other women in the world. . . . I've no place in life—no part in it. No duty. I'm a mere *thing*.'

The difference between them was quite bridged over, now that instead of words the subtler language of emotion had come into play. Mrs. Thomson knelt, looking petulantly at the fire; and for sole answer, the old housekeeper caressed her hand.

When at last Mrs. Thomson turned her face, her

eyes were glistening wet. She put up her other hand to take Mrs. Clarke's, and said: 'Do you think me very discontented and selfish? I was forgetting the trouble you have had. But, you see, it has made you kinder and better than me.'

The old woman's voice shook a little. 'Don't say that, ma'am. But I *do* think you're spared a good deal. And perhaps I am, too. . . . If the Lord had spared my own two boys, they might have grown up to be a trouble.'

As the only answer was a pressure of her hand, she went on softly: 'I don't know how it might have been with one of my own. But Doctor Mitchell seems almost like my own boy.'

Mrs. Thomson took away her hands and, smiling, said, '*He* doesn't make you sad?'

The old lady shook her head. 'Since we've been here in London—I don't know—I almost wish he'd get married. Though I don't hardly know how I should bear it.'

'But why, Mrs. Clarke? But why?' She stood up, smoothing down her dress; and then, taking hold of the mantelpiece, remained looking down at the fire.

Mrs. Clarke answered: 'You know I lived in London some years, while he was studying. I was in a big house. And some of the rich ladies there were—well, they were no better than they should be.'

'Oh, but surely . . .' The idea was too preposterous. Mrs. Thomson could hardly conceal a smile. 'Doctor Mitchell doesn't know any such people?'

'Doesn't he?'

'Why, who then?—And besides, if he does, he's not a simpleton.'

The old woman sighed, unconvinced. 'No; only, he's got no religion. That do trouble me. And he's so kind-hearted. . . . Sometimes I can't help wishing he was married.' She stood up, wrapping up her needlework.

This time Mrs. Thomson made no further effort to keep her. But, as she helped her visitor put on her mantle, she said: 'Very likely he may meet with some good woman while he's in London.'

With the words, a hope sprang up in her that perhaps her own niece might be the chosen woman; and when she was left alone, the hope developed far. Her niece's children would be—only less dear than children of her own would have been.

Mrs. Clarke, meanwhile, was only partially reassured. 'Poor thing!' she thought: 'she means well, I do think. But I hope she don't talk like that to him.'

Later in the evening, Mitchell was called in to Thomson's house. 'Mr. Hartmann,' the servant said, 'had come home with influenza.' On the following morning, the pretty servant too was down with it. Mrs. Thomson had no time for indulging day-dreams now. A strange exultation filled her at having something to do that seemed worth doing. Of the disorder she had no personal dread; but a strong physical loathing of it, laying its evil grip on thousands. To be combating it gave her the satisfaction of feeling in touch with other men and women—a feeling that was ennobled for her when she saw the suffering girl's eyes light up with confidence in the doctor, and heard his grave advice given for herself and her husband. His manner, and his occupation too, seemed to embody, somehow, that force of which she had been dimly conscious while Mrs. Clarke was with her that afternoon.

IX

ONE morning, calling to see Hartmann and the maidservant before starting on his longer rounds, Mitchell was let in by Mrs. Thomson herself.

'Do you mind waiting two or three minutes, doctor? I want to run upstairs before you go up; and there's my big boy must be got out of the way.' She showed him into the room where her husband had just risen from breakfast, saying to the latter, 'I'll bring your boots in a minute.' The 'big boy' greeted Mitchell in his most expansive manner, asking, 'When are you going to cure those poor wretches upstairs, my friend?'

The doctor laughed, answering, with an air of businesslike calculation: 'This is Monday... Tuesday ... Wednesday—I should think about Thursday.'

'Can't you hurry it up? Double their doses?'

'Hardly.... You see, that would profit the chemist more than me.'

Thomson laughed. 'Double your attendance too man; only get it over.... The house is all at sixes and sevens. And my wife...'

'She's looking uncommonly well,' interposed Mitchell.

'My dear fellow, she's actually enjoying herself.'

'What a confounded shame of her!'

Thomson looked more and more comically puzzled. 'I can't understand it,' he said.

'What can't you understand?' asked his wife, entering and placing the boots in his hand.

Taking them absently from her, he eyed her and replied slowly, 'Why, that'—he sat down deliberately, and drawing on one boot continued,—'that my clever wife should take delight in gruel and mustard-plasters, and generally in feeding and waiting upon the helpless.'

'I haven't fed you on mustard-plasters!'

'No . . . it's plain bread-and-butter nowadays. . . . I believe, Mitchell, that I ought to forbid . . . Dear! dear! there goes a shoe-lace. . . . What the deuce! Hurry up and find another, Nan! We're hindering the doctor. . . .' Flushed in the face, he looked up at Mitchell, and then, watching his wife, proceeded calmly: 'I was about to remark, Mitchell, that my wife will probably turn into a pillar of salt, or something of that order. She has put her hand to the plough, and is now turning back and taking delight in domesticity: although theoretically she holds that a woman's life ought not to be thrown away on such frivolities.'

The wife, who, having taken the boot out of her husband's hands, had found a lace and was quickly replacing it for the broken one, laughingly rejoined: 'Fred's theory differs from his practice, doctor. You see what he really desires. But you should have heard his praise of the runaway wife in last night's play. I believe he was in love with the heroine. . . . And now *I'm* lectured for staying at home to get his bread-and-butter!'

She finished a little petulantly; but he only smiled drily, saying: 'You are confusing the issues, my dear. I admire the plays, apart from the persons in them. You never will understand that.' Then, lacing his boot, while the others stood watching him, 'Still, there was much to be said for last night's heroine.' He stood up, and exchanging his quiet tone for one of briskness, almost of anxiety, added: 'Now, Edith's train is 8.3, isn't it? . . . I'll meet that, and you don't want me earlier, do you?'

She laughed: 'No, pray stay away.' Whereat he turned to Mitchell, trying to look dismal, and said: 'Do you see? . . . There's an example of what domesticity can bring a wife to.'

Although she replied lightly enough, Mitchell observed that she took a deep breath before saying: 'Go along and amuse yourself. If I were to run away, you wouldn't care—to judge by your talk.'

Thomson, with a 'Good-bye, Mitchell,' hurried away. Mrs. Thomson closed the door, and turned to Mitchell: 'Now, doctor, I won't keep you. *Isn't* he helpless?'

As he was leaving after seeing the two patients, he asked: 'But, I say, how is it? Where's the woman who's been helping you?'

Her smile was a trifle wearied. 'I sent her back at once. Influenza. . . . And there's been no time to find any one to help.'

'And Fred's let you? . . .' But ere he could finish, with a strange expression, that was partly friendship and partly anger, in her eyes, she placed her fingers before his mouth, almost touching him. 'You mustn't,' she said. Then, smiling: 'I don't want him at home to-day of all days. My niece is to come to-night; and I must prepare her room.'

'Don't knock yourself up.' Mitchell's voice was grave. She had not answered the objection he was about to have made to Fred's helplessness; but that she had not ignored it her eyes told him, forbidding him, too, to pursue the subject. A little nervously she said: 'I am really very well, and will take care. Perhaps you know of some woman who would help?'

'I'll see. . . .' While he was meditating, she bethought herself.

'The poor woman said she couldn't afford to go to a doctor. Will you forgive me? I promised that you should call. She didn't like to ask. . . . But I knew I had only to ask you.'

'Of course I'll go. Where does she live?'

The address was given. 'There are two or three others quite close,' he said.

'I guessed as much from the way she spoke of you. You are a good man, doctor.'

He smiled. 'And you are . . .' But she quickly interposed to finish his sentence—'learning the beauty of usefulness.'

The thought of her own new pleasure in being practically useful added happiness to her face. But he, with masculine egoism, found in her speech and expression a veiled compliment which he hastened to return. 'Don't depise the usefulness of beauty,' he said.

She was not thinking of compliments, and misunderstood. 'You mustn't be sarcastic at Fred's expense. An artist *can't* be useful. Besides'—with an uneasy laugh—'the husband is what the wife makes of him.'

'And if the converse is true?' he suggested, watching her face with secret admiration.

'Oh—he has little to be proud of in what he has made of me—if that were true. . . . But now I'm making *you* idle.'

He hurried off at her hint, or he might have spoken foolishly. But all day he was smiling to think how his light-heartedness might be taken as a proof of the useful power of her beauty. And at times, against his will, he wondered what Mrs. Thomson would have been with a husband less egoistic than Fred, or if she would indeed have made himself as useless as that singular man. Her apparent discontent gave him an uncomfortable feeling of neglected responsibility, which he lacked the time to analyse.

Three hours after his departure, a woman announced herself at Mrs. Thomson's. Doctor Mitchell had sent her, she said. She had been under his hands herself, and since he refused to make a charge, she was only too glad to come. Later in the day, Mrs. Clarke appeared. 'The doctor,' she explained, 'asked me if I could manage to look round and see if you wanted any help.' The old lady's manner betrayed so much unwillingness, that Mrs. Thomson was rejoiced to be able to tell her of the help that had already arrived. It seemed odd that this rather increased Mrs. Clarke's coolness. Fortunately for Mrs. Thomson, she was too busy to think of such matters.

X

By the Thursday, both Hartmann and the housemaid were considerably better, as Mitchell had promised that they should be. He didn't go near them, Lane Thomson having met him in the morning and given a favourable report. 'But,' Thomson said, 'you ought to come in to hear Edith's playing. Splendid is really not too good a word for it. . . . But then—she practises. She's at it all day, in fact.'

'How nice for my patients!' said Mitchell, thinking, however, of Thomson's wife, who hadn't time to practise.

Thomson's thin lips curled pleasantly. 'When will you recognise that people who are well are more worth considering than people who are sick?'

In the same cool, philosophical tone, but more ironically, Mitchell answered: 'When I've time to leave off living, and take to theories—and art.'

'Oh, but I am talking of Nature. Nature, you know, only values health.'

'I see. Then, whenever you need my help, you'll expect it in the form of poison — to accelerate Nature's work?'

Thomson smiled his appreciation, murmuring: 'Thou art not far from the kingdom of God. But my wife might object. One must consider her.'

'Must one? . . . Besides, she need not know. I could do it quite safely and secretly.'

Thomson laughed. 'I'll consider it. But'—for the other was turning away—'will you come in and have supper to-night?'

'Possibly . . . if I'm not very late home. I get to bed now as soon as I can after I have done.'

'What a dog's life!' Thomson smiled, on top of a yawn.

'Give me credit for being useful. . . . Say, a horse's life.'

'As you like. We'll see if we can get some beans or corn for your supper.'

. . . . .

Mitchell went to supper, and made the acquaintance of Miss Edith Sanderson. He also made a hole in his manners. For having a very easy chair set for him, where he could see her at the piano, he forgot to listen to the music, and noticing that she had decidedly pretty wrists and a pleasing shape, fell asleep smiling. Presently he began to be aware of talk. Thomson was saying gently: 'You would not suppose him to be a ferocious man, would you? yet this morning he was threatening to poison me!'

The doctor opened his eyes. The others were laughing, and he asked coolly: 'Is that why you invited me here, Thomson?—so that you could hocus the wine? Or'—he turned to the hostess—'was the drug in the salad? Anyhow, it wasn't strong enough. I've merely had a pleasant sleep.'

'Yes; you see, I didn't want to lose you, doctor,' laughed Mrs. Thomson.

With assumed jealousy her husband complained: 'You didn't consider his designs upon me! But I suppose you could spare me.'

The girl at the piano looked astonished, and with a mischievous glance at her Mrs. Thomson rejoined:

'You were teaching me to spare you all last week. And now that I have Edith. . . .'

Edith rose and left the piano. Was she mortified with him? Mitchell hoped not; but he knew that her playing would send him to sleep again. 'I've had about fifteen hours' sleep in the last three days,' he explained, as he shook hands with her and said good-night.

Her forgiving smile set him wondering, when they had parted, whether the aunt or the niece were the handsomer. Possibly the latter. Her high white forehead with fine hair drawn back from it, and her steely blue eyes with their quiet, truthful expression, took hold of his fancy. Yet, by way of doing justice to the earlier friend, on reaching home he glanced at her photograph. 'I *must* get a frame for this,' he muttered, replacing it in the drawer. And he added, 'Thomson is really a bit too unconcerned about her.'

The weather improving, the servant was well enough by Saturday to go home for a few days; and on the Sunday, Hartmann was recovered so far that Mitchell said he might go to work on the following day. This permission was given while they were having supper.

'Make it Tuesday, not to-morrow,' pleaded Hartmann.

'No; I protest, doctor,' said Lane Thomson, 'against your encouraging his laziness. In the name of the British tax-payer defrauded of his services, I protest. The empire may go to pieces for all he cares.'

'Why, then,' laughed Mitchell, 'I command him to do the duty England expects of him to-morrow.'

'Won't you plead for me, Miss Sanderson?' said Hartmann lugubriously.

The girl looked at her aunt laughingly. 'We don't encourage idleness, do we?'

Mrs. Thomson replied demurely, addressing Mitchell: 'It isn't idleness, doctor, but selfishness. He wants a good excuse for not going to the Spencers' to-morrow evening.'

'Oh—I *see*. That alters the case.... Well, Hartmann, have a previous engagement to dinner with me to-morrow.'

'Doctor Mitchell,' Thomson mocked, 'you shock me. Yesterday Mr. Spencer told me that you promised to be there to-morrow.'

At Mitchell's sigh and his dismal expression the others laughed. 'I had forgotten. I *did* promise,' he admitted; 'so I shall have to insist on your coming too, Hartmann.'

Hartmann began to look nettled. 'I'm not going,' he said shortly.

Mrs. Thomson's eyes flashed, but she spoke quietly to her husband: 'You and Doctor Mitchell must take care that your stories agree with the excuse he sends.'

Thomson laughed. 'Oh, we'll leave all that to you.'

She rejoined coolly: 'I shall have to stay at home to get his supper.'

'No; I won't have that!' exclaimed Hartmann. He looked a little indignant, and spoke reproachfully.

'You'll have to, if you stay at home,' she said decidedly.

The niece blushed slightly. 'Couldn't I do it, auntie? I don't know the Spencers.'

Her uncle's insinuating rejoinder, 'No; evidently you do *not* know Mrs. Spencer, or you wouldn't propose such a thing,' caused her to blush deeper still.

'I should like to be useful and helpful to Aunt Annie,' she urged.

But he: 'No; leave that to her. You do much better to be ornamental.' He continued: 'In short, you must come, Edith. You can't be spared. Your aunt may do as she likes. And I fancy, Nan, you'd not be sorry to have a good excuse for staying away?'

'Who would?' interposed the doctor, shrugging his shoulders; while Hartmann, with a gleam of fun in his eyes, said: 'Come now, Mrs. Thomson. What do you say to that? I'll be unfit to go out to-morrow evening, if you like.'

Mitchell laughed to her across the table: 'It's a fair offer, Mrs. Thomson.'

She was leaning back in her chair. Without condescending to notice Hartmann, she replied to Mitchell: 'Don't *you* encourage him, doctor. It is mere selfishness in him.'

Clasping his hands, Hartmann leaned over the table as though to argue with her. 'But, Mrs. Thomson,' he said, 'why should one go to see people he doesn't want to see, and who are sure to bore him?'

Thomson, with a glad expression of amusement, signed to Mitchell to hold his peace; and the lady began, looking sideways at Hartmann, 'If you let kindness bore you, Mr. Hartmann . . .'

Her husband interrupted, red-faced and eager: 'But confess, Nan, you will be horribly bored yourself?'

She turned to him. 'I confess it . . . but I'm ashamed of it.' Her colour was rising.

'And so you'll go as an act of penance?' persisted Hartmann.

'I shall go,' she said calmly—'that is, if you don't stay at home—because Mrs. Spencer takes a lot of trouble to please us, and it isn't kind to stay away.' She stood up, the meal being ended. 'It's really to please Fred that I go there.'

Her husband sat looking up at her, and putting on an amused expression that annoyed Mitchell, who turned to Hartmann angrily, when the latter anticipated any remonstrance by saying, 'Oh, very well. I'll go.'

'You needn't to please me,' said Mrs. Thomson, stooping to stir the fire.

A shade of annoyance came over her husband's face. 'What a complicated and unsatisfactory business you make of it,' he said, 'trying to please other people instead of yourselves.'

'I know. It isn't easy to please *you*,' the wife said perversely.

'You shouldn't try.' He had risen, and put his hand on her arm. But she turned pettishly from him. He went on, good-humouredly: 'You really needn't go if it's only for my sake, Nan.'

To Mitchell's lips leapt a question: 'Then why need Edith?' utterance to which, he was afterwards glad to think, had been prevented by the lady's objection, made with a sudden penitent glance at her husband: 'I'm afraid they'd be vexed if I didn't go.'

Was it, Mitchell wondered, the suspicion of tears

in her eyes that made Thomson turn away, saying peevishly, 'That's a way of looking at it which I never can understand.'

The lady's chin lifted. She placed a tray on the table, and began putting their glasses on it, while she rejoined: 'I know you can't. Nor Mr. Hartmann. Perhaps Doctor Mitchell can. If you'll go into the other room, Edith will play to you while I put away the supper.'

Thomson squared his shoulders gallantly and good-temperedly before her, and, laughingly taking her by the arm, said: 'Ask Mitchell to help you; and then you can talk to him too.'

The doctor, just behind him, saw her grow very red, trying to free herself. In an instant, muttering, 'Come along, you idiot!' he clutched Thomson's other elbow.

Those who had ever experienced Mitchell's grip remembered it. Thomson turned. 'Ao—w, you villain! I believe you've broken my arm.'

'Be thankful it wasn't your head, man.'

Silently Edith had begun to help her aunt.

'Do you know, Edith,' Thomson said, 'why Doctor Mitchell is like a dishonest glazier?'

The girl glanced up with a shy laugh, and Mitchell said, 'Come along, man! we're blocking the way.' His fingers touched the other's elbow again.

At that, pursued by the doctor and the women's exclamations, Thomson made an undignified dash for the other room. There Hartmann was already lighting a cigarette. As the others followed his example, he looked at them with an embarrassed smile, saying, 'I feel rather sat upon, Thomson.'

'Serve you right,' said Mitchell provokingly.

Thomson, with the match at his cigarette, lifted his brows in a despondent way, and raised his shoulders in the manner of a man who thinks more than he cares to say. His only words were, 'It isn't safe to disagree with Mitchell.' Then he rubbed his elbow, smiling upon the doctor.

Hartmann frowned. 'It seems so unreasonable to go fooling off there to-morrow night. And yet Mrs. Thomson makes me feel like a sneak, none the less.'

'My dear boy, you'll learn to live down those feelings when you've a wife and domestic cares.' Then fretfully, 'I thought Edith was coming,' he said, and closed the door, as if eager to shut out the reproachful sounds of domestic work that came from the supper-room.

XI

WHEN dinner was announced at Spencer's the fact that Mitchell had not arrived was evidently distressing to the host and hostess. To Mrs. Thomson's suggestion, 'He ought to come in time,' Mrs. Spencer said gravely, 'Oh—but a doctor, my dear!' Her husband had drawn hesitating comfort from Hartmann's assurance that Mitchell didn't much care what he ate, so long as he got enough. Miss Sanderson, on Hartmann's arm, glanced grave amusement from her pale grey eyes. He emphasised the statement, and seeing that it pleased her to think of Mitchell as a kind of beneficent barbarian, he went on at table to tell them how Mitchell had positively enjoyed the recent frost, and had boasted only that morning of a kind of delight in spending night and day at work.

'It *pays* him, you know,' suggested Mrs. Thomson with pretended contempt, so astonishing to Hartmann that he began, 'Oh! but, hang it! . . .'

Mrs. Thomson smiled. He looked at Miss Sanderson, and was rewarded by a 'You're a true friend, Mr. Hartmann,' that no one else heard.

Mrs. Spencer was saying, 'He ought to be thankful for such good health.'

'I've no doubt he is,' said Thomson solemnly.

The others smiled, but the hostess's grey head shook reproof. 'I'm afraid you don't mean it, Mr. Thomson.' But she had heard that Mitchell was very good to the poor (here Hartmann murmured to Miss Sanderson that he could tell a thing or two about that), and no doubt they needed it. A gruesome account of distress, quoted from that day's paper, followed at unappetising length. Lane Thomson shrugged his shoulders, with a sly grimace towards his wife. Hartmann shivered, and agreed with Miss Sanderson's murmur, 'I hate to think about it.' Mr. Spencer expostulated gently with his wife, and Mrs. Thomson, her cheeks flushed, murmured, 'What a snob Nature is!' to be followed by her husband's glad 'Very good, Nan! But I shouldn't have thought it of you.'

Mrs. Spencer began, 'Is it quite right to talk like that?'

'Oh, but, Mrs. Spencer, look! Nature—the winter—asks, *Do you wear gloves?* I show mine. Nature cringes away, finds some ragged child or other, and pinches its hands with chilblains, because it doesn't wear gloves.'

'Very good, Nan! But you'll have Mitchell down on you if you talk against Nature.'

'But, uncle,' the girl began.

'But, Edith,' he interrupted, 'don't commit yourself. Mitchell will tell you that Nature is not to blame.'

'Yes; but *we*'re not Nature.'

'Very true,' murmured Hartmann, and Mrs. Spencer took up the parable. She thought the well-to-do at fault. We should be more charitable. 'Mr. Spencer insisted, when he was ill last winter, upon giving to the poor a penny for every penny that was spent upon himself.'

As if he would say, 'I don't know *why* I did it,' Mr. Spencer looked apologetically at Thomson, who merely twinkled back his amusement, while Mrs. Thomson patted the old man's hand sympathetically; and Mrs. Spencer was still damping all their spirits when Mitchell arrived.

The hope with which all greeted him was disappointed. He seemed depressed, and soon their hostess was asking him, 'Didn't he think himself privileged in being able to serve the poor—to show his sympathy *practically*?'

To Thomson's disappointment he avoided the pitfall, and answered moodily, 'I'd rather see them help themselves.'

Mrs. Thomson, who was sitting next to him, said demurely, 'I'm afraid you don't look at it in quite the right spirit, doctor.' Mrs. Spencer added, a little severely, 'I should think it a great privilege, if I were

F

you.' The girl remarked, with a shy smile, 'Doctor Mitchell's only modest, perhaps.'

As the doctor merely shook his head, Thomson laughed flippantly. '*You*'ll never be accused of modesty,' suggested Hartmann.

'I'm ashamed of him,' said Mrs. Thomson. '*I* agree with Mrs. Spencer.'

'But I suppose,' smiled Spencer, trying to divert the conversation into a less personal channel, 'you don't think the poor a kind of blessing—a mere field for developing our own virtues?'

'Nobody would think *that*,' said his wife severely.

'On the contrary, I could show you the idea in a dozen books.'

'Ah, *books*! But let's be practical.' Mrs. Thomson shot an understanding glance at her husband as she spoke.

'Yes,' said Mrs. Spencer. 'We don't know *why* there are poor; but we know it's our duty to help them.'

Mitchell's face grew yet more gloomy; and Hartmann, observing it, asked, 'Don't you think so, doctor?'

Mitchell looked up drearily. 'Do *you* think so?' And again Thomson laughed, with aggravating enjoyment of the curious entertainment they were having.

Hartmann smiled warily. 'Ask me again—when I've studied political economy.'

'Yes; it's a question for economists,' said old Mr. Spencer with a sigh.

'And meanwhile . . .' Miss Sanderson began.

'Meanwhile the poor must wait.' Mitchell spoke almost brutally.

Mrs. Thomson pounced on him. 'And the doctors take holiday, I suppose?'

'He didn't say that, aunt.'

Mrs. Spencer returned to her point. 'I think it's a question of duty, not of science.'

Mrs. Thomson supported her. 'We women believe in con-science, don't we, Mrs. Spencer?'

'Spare us, Nan! Or at least have a little pity on language!'

'It's more than you have on the poor.'

'Your "conscience" should remind you of your duty to your husband. But I notice that about conscience—that it is kept for other people's benefit.'

'You don't keep one for the benefit of the poor.'

The men laughed. But 'Oh, hush, my dear,' said Mrs. Spencer.

'I'd better explain,' said Thomson. 'You know, I don't much approve of doctors.' Mitchell merely glanced at him with an amused but tired smile. 'Practical people take a lot of trouble—like Mitchell here—and it's mostly wasted. His patients linger on till next year, instead of dying out of the way. I take no trouble. But I encourage what is strong to be stronger, and what is excellent to be more excellent. Sickness never breeds beauty. I don't care about the sick or the poor. I like the well, and the thriving, and the clever; and I spend my money on their pictures and books.

'How extremely altruistic!'

At the wife's sarcasm, Mr. Spencer smiled. 'There's reason in it, Mrs. Thomson.' He glanced at her niece, and his face lit up. But it was not of pretty girls that he spoke. 'A good horse, you know, doesn't come from doctoring up the old diseased raw-boned specimens. These may only spoil the breed. You must cherish what is good, and let the rest go. I'm sorry,' he added, in response to his wife's look of contempt, 'but it is so.'

'There's no denying it,' Mitchell said. 'I've done no good of that sort to-day.'

'Do you agree with them, Mr. Hartmann?' asked Miss Sanderson.

'It seems all right, doesn't it?' he admitted reluctantly.

'It seems so unkind,' she objected.

Mrs. Spencer wished that men would not talk so foolishly.

'So *wickedly*,' urged Mrs. Thomson, with impressive gravity. 'I *know* Fred's wicked. Mr. Hartmann isn't much better. And I begin to doubt Doctor Mitchell.'

Again the men laughed. Miss Sanderson looked puzzled, but Mrs. Spencer said, 'I think you talk rather extravagantly, my dear. They don't *mean* wrong, I hope.'

'Do you exempt me?' asked their host.

'Not wholly. But you are not so unnatural. . . .'

Thomson laughed. 'I hoped you'd use the word. You know, Mitchell, she's been telling us that Nature is a snob.'

'Rank blasphemy!' laughed Mitchell.

'And if we're unnatural, we're *not* snobs, I suppose?'

'I said nothing of *Human* Nature,' Mrs. Thomson rejoined quickly.

'That doesn't help you, Mrs. Thomson,' laughed Hartmann. 'Human nature is snobbish enough.'

'True! True!' Thomson cried.

'Yours, if you like.' She paid no heed to Mrs. Spencer's 'Hush!' but continued gaily, 'Not Mr. Spencer's, nor Mrs. Spencer's, nor Edith's.'

Mr. Spencer smiled. 'There are two sides to Human Nature. We've all got the snobbish side; but there's the kindly, too.'

'Artificial,' Thomson objected, laughingly.

'Oh!—not *kindness*, uncle!' Miss Sanderson flushed as Hartmann echoed, 'No, not kindness.'

Mitchell spoke bitterly, 'I don't observe that it's very *natural*.'

Mrs. Spencer suggested reverently, 'May it not be supernatural, doctor? The poor . . .'

'O Mrs. Spencer, I'm sick of the poor to-day!'

'For shame! doctor. But you're tired, and want a smoke. We'll leave you.'

At the door, Mrs. Thomson said: 'I hope, Fred, that you've got something to ask Mr. Spencer about. At any rate, don't hurry. The doctor and Mr. Hartmann may come soon.'

She followed her hostess, gaily humming. And to the elder lady's remark, 'I think you try his temper very much,' she laughed, 'You mustn't take me seriously. *He* never does!' She frowned down her niece's astonished look, and began to talk with almost feverish lightness, affecting not to see the occasional sad shaking of Mrs. Spencer's head. 'My own temper seems touchy, I admit.' Here she laughed. 'I'm nearly cross. Are you cross, Edith? If you're not, I shall be crosser. It's the weather. This damp, warm, spring weather, come so suddenly, tries one's nerves. I suppose that's partly what it's for, don't you think? I don't *blame* the weather. That would be what they call—*Manicheism*, wouldn't it? When I was a little girl, I remember laying the blame of my bad temper on the rainy day. They told me that *I* was to blame; that it was the devil in me; and I said, "I always thought it was conscience *in* me, and . . ."'

'But—my dear, my dear.' Mrs. Spencer could not endure this talk. Fortunately, at this moment, the two younger men came in. Eagerly Mrs. Thomson began: 'O doctor, don't you think this weather very trying to the temper? *Do* say it is!'

This mood of hers was strange to him. He glanced with surprise at her flushed cheeks, and nervously glistening eyes, then at Mrs. Spencer's frown. Smiling, he replied, 'I don't know. I'm afraid my temper hasn't been quite blameless. Will you forgive me, Mrs. Spencer? I'll be good now.'

He had taken the old lady's two hands. Her answer was a friendly pressure, and a lenient 'Charity covers a multitude of sins, doctor. Now we'll try to make you forget your tiring day. What do you say, Edith?' She looked meaningly towards the piano.

The girl laughed, blushing a little; and Hartmann laughed too, exclaiming, 'That's the way to send him to sleep.'

His former misdemeanour had to be explained. Mrs. Spencer shook her head at him playfully, and asked, 'What would *you* like, doctor?' But it was the niece who replied, questioning her aunt, 'Won't you sing to us?'

Mrs. Thomson blushed. 'I can't, can I, Mr. Hartmann?'

'You've never let me hear you.'

Mitchell remembered that she had once sung to him. Now she gave him one look. He ignored that previous evening, and said merely, 'I wish you'd let us hear you now'; and he felt that her immediate consent was a special favour to himself.

They had asked for her first song again; and she was already half-way through it, when the other two men came in. At sight of her husband she stopped, flushed, and left the piano.

'Go on, Nan. Don't mind me,' he said quickly. The others, too, protested. 'You *must* hear it, Henry!' said Mrs. Spencer, making room for her husband on the sofa, where she took his hand, with a look at Thomson that meant—'This is how husband and wife should be.'

Mrs. Thomson tried again; but now her voice refused obedience to her will.

'Hang it, Thomson!' began Mitchell, 'why the ... why couldn't you stay away a little longer?'

The lady interposed laughingly. 'Fred doesn't like me to sing. He says my voice is better the less I practise it.'

Mitchell, lolling back in his easy chair, muttered, 'In that, it resembles my temper, Mrs. Thomson.' He shut his eyes and stretched out his legs. 'Play me to sleep if you can, Miss Sanderson. I'm tired.'

His suddenly affected weariness was annoying, and the more because, in spite of the music, he seemed nervously restless. But in the intervals, the evening was saved—if saved it was—by Thomson's urbanity and the flow of gay, frivolous talk that he assisted his wife to maintain. Gradually, too, Mitchell recovered his tone; and he was joking with the rest when they set off to walk the half-mile or so to the district station.

XII

TO neither Hartmann nor Mitchell, walking in the rear with Miss Sanderson between them, was it pleasing that Mrs. Thomson suddenly turned round with a 'Don't you think so, Mr. Hartmann?' compelling him to leave the doctor and the girl alone. 'Why couldn't she ask Mitchell?' he grumbled to himself. Mitchell, too, wondered why not. In the latter part of the evening she had shown him so much favour that he had forgotten until now how she had disagreed with him at dinner. Was she unwilling to be left alone with her husband? Or afraid that himself would take the husband to task on the subject of her singing? Pondering these things, he had almost forgotten his companion, until she suddenly halted, and stooped with her foot on a doorstep. 'My shoe-lace is undone,' she said, breaking their long silence. He bent to assist her, catching a glimpse of an ankle that made him forgetful of his other thoughts; but, before she could possibly have tied the lace—if it really was undone—she stood up, assuring him that it was all right. The slight delay had allowed the other three to get forward well out of ear-shot.

He was thinking of the ankle, and of the shoulder so close beside him, when she startled him with a question: 'Doctor Mitchell—don't let us catch up—do you know what is the matter with my aunt? Is there *any*thing? Twice to-night, when she thought no one was looking, I saw her put her hand to her side and breathe as if it hurt her. And she looked unhappy, until she caught me watching.'

'And then I suppose she grimaced? No?'

'Did she to you?' the girl asked.

He ignored her question, saying, 'I think she was only bored to death. Weren't you?'

'Not exactly *bored*,' she said dubiously.

'Nor yet amused?'

'Certainly not.' Her laugh was disdainful.

'What, then?'

'Oh,—I can't tell you.'

'*I* get horribly sick of the poor old lady.'

'Do you? I didn't mind her.' Miss Sanderson spoke with cool tolerance.

'Perhaps Hartmann wearied you? He *can* be tedious, at times.'

'Oh, who takes any notice of Mr. Hartmann?'

She may have fancied that she had spoken too feelingly, for she hurried into the explanation that a minute earlier she had said she couldn't make. 'No; I was put out with uncle—with Mr. and Mrs. Thomson.... Why do they do it?'

Mitchell suggested: 'You know, in company, people like to hide their real feelings under a mask....' Hesitating, he had forced a laugh that spoilt the effect of what he had said. The girl sighed; 'I don't know....' But Mitchell, disliking perhaps to hear his own suspicions formulated, interrupted. 'I think very likely Mrs. Thomson is pulled down with nursing Hartmann and the servant. A change would do her good.'

'I could keep house if she went away. I wish

you'd try to persuade her. I'm sure you've got a lot of influence with her.'

Evidently this young lady had keen powers of observation. Hitherto, her collected manner, her quietness, even the scarlet of her thin curving lips, had suggested to him something gracefully statuesque, and delicately tinted. Now in the darkness he remembered the light in her grey eyes; and hoped for the lighted railway carriage, and the chance it might afford of seeing the effects of animation in her face.

But as the train came in, Thomson said, 'Do you mind smoke, Edith?' For answer, she jumped into the smoking-carriage, while her uncle held the door. Hartmann followed. Mrs. Thomson, shaking her head distastefully, got into the next compartment. 'Do you care about smoking, Mitchell?' Thomson asked. 'I'll take care of your wife for you,' was the reply. 'Well, birds of a feather,' said Thomson genially. The doors were slammed, and the doctor found himself sitting opposite Mrs. Lane Thomson. But for those two, the compartment was empty.

Mitchell sat down in the corner opposite to his companion. 'You shouldn't have troubled about me,' she said, 'why didn't you go and have a smoke?'

He shrugged his shoulders. 'They'll be talking about music, or art. I don't care about it.'

She smiled languidly, and, taking off her hat, leaned her head back in the corner of the carriage. 'It was very nice of you to come,' she said; and shut her eyes.

Mitchell might have inferred that her husband's leaving her alone was not so nice. He noticed the brown hair waving over her temples, and softly shaking to the train's rattle. The smile left her lips; she frowned slightly; yet Mitchell, watching her with a sense of not having before seen her—her eyes, when open, challenged all your attention if you could endure them at all—traced, now that the eyes' darkness was veiled, an unsuspected likeness to Edith in her other features, well lit from the central lamp above. How could her husband leave such a woman to travel in loneliness? But now the frown was passing again. She had something to say.

Opening her eyes, 'How do you like Edith?' she asked. 'Don't you think she's very nice?'

'I was thinking that she's very much like you.'

Was thinking. That meant, *was looking*. She didn't shut her eyes again, but, the bright excitement of her colour increasing almost imperceptibly, she said, 'That isn't an answer to my question.' Then she blushed with vexation at seeming to ask for a compliment.

Smiling, he rejoined, 'I'm afraid I mustn't answer now.'

Her eyelids lowered, with an alertly defensive expression; and, gazing at him so, she said quietly, 'No compliments, *please*. I'm sick of idle talk,'—adding, as though half unwillingly—'like we've had to-night.'

'Indeed? And I was rather glad to see you apparently in such high spirits.'

'Do men ever see *any*thing beneath the surface?' She looked disconsolately into the darkness.

Then suddenly throwing her head back, and looking at him again, 'I'm disappointed in you,' she said, with a petulant laugh.

'I'm sorry to hear that.'

'I have been, all the evening. You shouldn't have backed up Fred and Hartmann, at dinner. Of course I could see something had vexed you, but still . . .'

His face clouded. She half hoped for an outburst of anger, but he spoke quietly: 'I had pulled two or three up from death's door. One was a drunkard —beats his wife, I suspect. Another was a girl . . . who'll live to wish she'd died. There are streets and streets full of misery, very likely, over our heads now.' As he spoke, there seemed something heartless in being whirled under it all in that gas-lit train. 'There's too much poverty. My work seemed useless.'

'And so you preferred our folly. It seemed dead to me: glittering death.'

'And yet you did it very well.'

'Oh, I *did* it! And hated it. I hate the cold, insincere, passionless life I'm living now. . . . I seem to have no genuine feeling for anything. It was only out of mockery that I pretended to back up Mrs. Spencer's talk of "duty." Even you men could see that, I suppose?'

Mitchell laughed gently, at the scorn of his sex, saying: 'Of course. I thought it was what the old lady deserved. She sickened me.'

'It was as good as your "philosophy" deserved. And I believe I hoped to provoke Fred, by not condescending to answer him better. Because, there is —or I used to think there was—a better answer. Like Mrs. Spencer's; only, somehow, *true*. Hers sounds so false. She's only got the words, and doesn't feel them. Nor I, either, nowadays.'

Mitchell sighed. 'I don't worry about it, you know. The best way is, to live your own life. . . .'

She interrupted: 'Oh, I know all that talk, and despise it.' She laughed contemptuously. 'You begin by showing that a woman's life with her husband is one-sided; and then you assume that mental one-sidedness is as ugly as physical. After that, you prove that the wife's duty is to leave her husband.'

'Well?' He smiled. 'You see, I'm talking to a wife.'

She was pleased to laugh at his adroitness: and went on more calmly, 'The logic of it is very good, I dare say. When Fred takes the part of the women in books,' she named several erratic heroines, 'I can't answer him, and yet . . . oh! I can't answer him; but for all that I know—or used to know . . .' She didn't finish her sentence, but leaned back in pure weariness, and again shut her eyes.

How had they digressed into this subject? When he remembered, Mitchell too leaned back to watch her. If, as she professed, she had no feeling left, what was giving that heightened colour to her face? And was Thomson to blame? or did she never speak so earnestly to him? At any rate, her state was unenviable now. By her breathing it was plain that her nerves were all a-quiver. No doctor's medicine could avail much—but a husband's arm. . . . Mitchell, with a glance of the thought at Edith in the next compartment, began dreamily to wish himself a husband, with a wife needing strong masculine support. 'Even little courtesies—the delicate deference of man to woman—would be so delicious,' he was thinking, when a sigh from his companion brought his mind back straight to her actual need.

'I oughtn't to bother you about these things,' she began.

But he, 'Why not? You're hot. It's close here. Shall we have the window open?'

Yes: she recognised his consideration. 'If you think best,' she said.

It was a little thing; but her manner encouraged him to try again. The wind entering, caught and lifted her hair. 'But you mustn't sit in a draught,' he said; 'let's change places.'

'And you?' she said, to his gratification, obeying him none the less willingly. It was touching to see her so readily appreciative of his attention. And it was but a kind of gas-lit, drawing-room courtesy, after all; not what she chiefly needed; not the high sympathy belonging to sunlight and the airy hills. Mitchell was conscious of his powerlessness to help her; but here, underground, whirling in a glare of light below a sleeping, uneasy cityful of men and women, no inspiration came to him. Stupidly he thought to soothe her with reasons; and presently, leaning forward, began—

'You don't bother me, you know. I'm as interested as you in self-development. I begin to wonder whether sticking to my work—you know it has been a kind of wife to me—mayn't cramp me. I don't want to be a specialist.'

'No? I've envied you. . . . I thought once . . . But what *do* you want?'

'You'll laugh. It has only come vividly since we've been here. . . . I should like to be married and have children, and live a jolly, smart, vivid life—full of gaiety and pleasure.'

'Ah—the children! I don't believe the rest.'

He smiled: 'Not the wife?'

Her replying laugh was a little disdainful. 'If she were good enough for you, she would keep you—help you. . . .'

Her hesitation, and the sudden flush accompanying it, were painful. Mitchell read her thought. What had she done, to keep her husband from playing with his life? He spoke hurriedly: 'Perhaps I shouldn't enjoy it. . . . But to-day's experience has rather upset me. My work seems worse than useless. . . .'

'But it's worth doing. And if you could find a woman to encourage you . . .'

He guessed what she would have said. Suddenly they became aware that the train had stopped at their station. They hurried out. The others were already far up the platform, and, seeing that they were following, passed on. As he took Mrs. Thomson's arm, Mitchell, thinking how with Edith's the pleasure would have been lawful, was acutely aware of the warmth beneath his companion's sleeve. Was it fair to her, to let her confide so much in him. A temptation to shock her into wariness by pressing her arm was with difficulty withstood. For safety, he heaved his thoughts bodily over to the fascinating subject of Edith's ankle; until naturally they travelled on to the task she had enjoined on him.

They were in the street. Hartmann's voice came back, followed by the girl's laugh, gay and lighthearted. Hartmann, then, could make her careless of her aunt's trouble? 'But I'm not indifferent to it,' thought Mitchell. He asked, 'Have you made up your mind to go for a holiday?'

To both of them there came back a vivid remembrance of the first time when he had advised her to have a change.

There was a slight tremor in her arm. 'You may be right, doctor. I told you I was disappointed, but—I fancy you understand. I'm out of sorts with myself. It may not be wise; but I'd sooner fight it out on the spot. It seems cowardly to run away. It's like you with your work. We must stick to it. I'm all right now, you see. A little exhibition of temper to you clears the air.'

At her door, where the other three were waiting, she resumed her gaiety. And with his good-tempered smile, her husband congratulated her. 'We owe this evening to you. Nothing but your good spirits saved us. It's rather an ordeal. If Spencer weren't so useful to me, I'd cut the connection.'

Edith Sanderson wondered why Mitchell shook his head meaningly, as he said good-night. His grip of her hand hurt her fingers: would they be stiff in the morning? 'You must come to me to cure them, if they are,' he said, with an accent of hope at which Mrs. Thomson smiled to herself.

In bed, he suddenly realised that it must have been moonlight that had shone on Edith's foot. But 'I'm hanged if I know whether it's a full moon, or what!' he murmured happily.

XIII

THAT geniality which had made Mitchell an admired favourite of the villagers of Rothwell hitherto had served him well in London. His newly-made friends remarked to one another that such a man was wasted in the country, and they gently urged him to relinquish all thoughts of returning to Rothwell at the year's end. Yet, although admittedly tempted, he shook his head. There was something —he could not explain what—that told him it would not do. The friends, therefore, continued to urge him.

He could not explain, because he was unaware of the conditions on which his character rested. Apart from his own native tendencies—the tendencies which had first attracted and since endeared Dr. Wright to him for so many years, there had been two great external influences moulding him. One was Wright's friendship, the other his profession. To these his character, like a climbing plant, had clung, nor as yet had cared to assert itself apart from them. It so well suited his disposition to practise a silent imaginative concern for other people's doings, and, in fact, to project himself into their interests, that he was content to forgo pleasures more personal to himself, such as would have disturbed his equanimity.

It was, in fact, largely owing to that long friendship of his that he had never been in love. For to a sensitiveness almost feminine, Wright joined a masculine strength—an incisiveness as well as a large grip—of intellect; and, beside that combination, all the women Mitchell had ever met seemed inferior. The woman he loved was an ideal never yet met. Yet—and thanks again partly to Wright— he had disdained any partial satisfaction, any indulgence in temporary passion or languid amour.

Pleasures so imperfect would only have sullied the more enduring joy that he had in sympathising with other people. Consequently he practised, readily enough, a self-effacement, an asceticism, which he was far from seeking to impose on other men. It enabled him not only to tolerate what he did not permit to himself, but even theoretically to share those paradoxes which are modern orthodoxy, in many matters of opinion. He was, in fact, in the world, and yet not of it.

In the same direction, he had been influenced by his work. He could do it the better by effacing himself and sharing the burdens of his patients. Much of the work demanded, too—and of a bachelor especially—a temperate and impersonal behaviour that is above suspicion. He needed to be a man whom women could trust as though he also were a woman. The sense of this trust bestowed upon him was a reward in itself—a priceless possession, not lightly to be thrown away for an unworthy gratification. It had sweetened and dignified the long summer evenings at Rothwell, filling them with luminous thoughts; and yet the experience gained in his work, and the knowledge that work required of him, had on its side made for tolerance. Before his coming to London, few men had been more contented than he. Solitude was congenial to a man 'living out of the world,' and not caring to enter it save by the one path which his profession opened to him.

But, that solitude lost, there had been going on within him a process of which he first became uneasily aware on the day of that visit to the

Spencers. In the first place, the helpless, seething misery of London poverty was sickening him. Thomson's theory that you should help the well rather than the ill touched a place already sore into an open wound. From dull wonder why those miserable people should wish to live, he passed rapidly into an intense conviction that they would be better dead. His work, still faithfully carried out, began to be no longer a joy but a contradiction—a dis-service rather than a service to mankind.

Old Mr. Spencer's talk about horses confirmed him in this view; and when he recalled it on the following day, it seemed to be a criticism on another part of his life.

For, in descending from his aloof position of sympathy, and endeavouring to live the same sort of life as was lived by his new friends, he found himself somehow in the background. He could not do it so well as they, while the effort cost him the peace which belongs to the mere looker-on, such as he had previously been. Without the loneliness of Rothwell, and amidst the rapid movement that was now dragging him along, a part of itself, he lost the old high-minded content and fellow-feeling; it was being exchanged for eagerness liable to degenerate into the fretful. He began to ask himself what good he was in the world if his profession was a mistake? and he began to fear that he had sunk the man in the physician. All those fine thoughts that once had satisfied him—they were sterile and worthless after all. Besides, he had seen them caricatured, as it were (just as Mrs. Lane Thomson had seen them), in the platitudes of old Mrs. Spencer.

Other questions inevitably began to formulate within him. Inevitably, since that profession, as one of the walls to which the climbing plant had grown, was threatening to crumble away from him, the need to assert himself grew more and more imperative. He remembered Wright's opinion, that a man unmarried was necessarily incomplete. He had always subscribed to that opinion, but never until lately had it seemed to affect him; never until now had it struck him that it was his own fault, and not the fault of fate, that had left him a bachelor at thirty-five. Now, however, he began to feel that he might be wrong, and to ask himself whether he was the master of his own life or a passionless fool of circumstance, rendered docile, even servile, by worn-out puritanical prejudice. These varied feelings were but waiting for his recognition. That walk home from the Spencers' gave to them the final shake which crystallised them gradually into conscious thoughts.

Edith Sanderson's ankle; the agile and delicate movement of her knee and waist as she straightened herself to resume her walk; the skirt falling almost foldless, and its rustling murmur to the girl's active step; then Mrs. Thomson's quivering need of man's comfort, and afterwards her soft arm touching his own confidingly,—of such things as this he had experience before, yet now recollection of them rioted in him. Through the white light of the masculine intellect the feminine shone in rosy emotion, sweetly defiant of the half-ascetic modesty which was the habit of a lifetime. And then there returned to his mind the prospect of married life, less frantic than when he spoke of it in the train, but more alluring. The incomplete man burned with desire for completeness—for wife and children, to save the worth and strength now wasting in him. He could make his wife so happy, so blessed, he knew, and himself too. A sickening fear rushed over him, that he might die without knowing the delirious joy of folding the one woman in his arms. It was horrible, and it was his own fault. He saw that his puritanical habit had nearly ruined his life.

He gave the habit evil names, regarding it as an effete tradition which he ought long ago to have spurned away as worthy only of the Dark Ages, when the body and its functions were feared along with a devil and a fiery hell. It was a treason against the world's life, a wanton murder of his own living forces, a kind of suicide, a blasphemy that called Good evil. How its existence had originated he did not consider. He despised the habit, and yet for a time it clung to him.

Still, he was slowly changing. One April morning he was startled into consciousness of that, when Lane Thomson's pretty servant blushed and gave him a coquettish 'Good-morning,' as he passed her while she was cleaning a window. Her lifted shoulder and bare arm were beautiful, but—to have shown his admiration was hardly desirable, or fair to the girl, who, he remembered, was a Rothwell girl, with a lucky lover in the old village.

This incident warned him that he had better be careful of his behaviour with Edith and her aunt. But in their society he was still happy enough to become unconscious of himself, as of old, so that he behaved with his old-fashioned habitual ease. Or if at times sudden thought reminded him to be defiant of that habit, it was only to be set wondering whether, after all, there might be the greater satisfaction in yielding to it.

Meanwhile, Lane Thomson's suave indifference irritated him more and more. If the man could not see the distress of which he seemed to be so often the cause, Mitchell felt that somehow he must enlighten him; for he was unwilling to believe that Thomson would be intentionally inconsiderate. Accordingly, he opposed the other's absurd opinions, not observing how bitter he himself was growing. Unfortunately, Thomson asked for reasons; and, as usually happens, Mitchell's reasons lagged far behind his convictions. Even to himself he could not explain what was so unsatisfying in his friend's æsthetics.

Of this particular puzzle, however, a solution at last dawned upon him, bringing with it a temporary peace. On the last Saturday evening in May, there called upon him the pretty housemaid's sweetheart, Joe Baker, from Rothwell. Mitchell insisted joyfully on finding him a bed. They had supper together, too. This young man's careless glance; the look of him, that had nothing to conceal, because his love was clean and his work a pleasure; the ripe sunburn, the richly-ringing dialect, and the talk of the haymaking; the half-fancied odour of cattle, which no honest soap will wash from off a farm-lad's hands, all gave a new turn to Mitchell's feelings. He envied the fellow that hardy life, where now the air was steeped in leagues of sunlight, and lapped clean and intoxicating over the waving grass in meadow and upland. And Joe brought with him—a gift from old Peter—the first picking of green peas in the village: Mitchell remembered the sowing of them in November, and appreciated the giver's pride. Old Peter, like young Joe, needed no Art: their life was sweet without it. How was this?

Late on Sunday evening, while the train was rattling Joe back home to the quiet of Rothwell, Hartmann and Mitchell were strolling through one of the Parks. Every seat was occupied by amorous couples, clasping one another round neck and waist. The sight had an aspect of shamelessness which Mitchell refused to recognise. At his friend's expression of disgust, he laughed. 'Why shouldn't they? It's nature. I think I like it.'

When they reached home, the remark was repeated to Thomson, who smiled his provoking smile, that made you uncertain how far he was treating you seriously. 'I suppose they've nothing better to do—except drink. Drunkenness and love-making are the British public's substitute for Art.' As he spoke and laughed, enjoyment seemed to radiate from his shining bald head.

'*That's* not love-making. It's . . .' Hartmann hesitated, his dark eyes resting on Edith Sanderson.

For one moment, Mitchell resented her presence that checked discussion. Then, at the open windows, the cool air of the summer night stirred the curtains. He glanced at Edith. . . . How if he were alone with her? . . . 'It's only love-making in public,' he hinted.

And Lane Thomson rejoined, 'Yes; I daresay

your friend Joe What's-'is-name and our girl have been at it.'

Miss Sanderson began to blush. No one noticed that her blush was simultaneous with Hartmann's sudden change of the conversation. He spoke of Joe appreciatively, yet half pityingly. 'He looks a clever fellow: too good for a bumpkin's life.'

Mrs. Thomson glanced aside at Hartmann's plate —they were having supper—to remark, 'No; it's for town-life that he's too good. What could he do with himself in London?'

'Why, flirt and drink,' her husband suggested mischievously.

Mitchell cried, so that Mrs. Thomson, who had been looking bored, glanced anxiously at him: 'You've given me an idea, Thomson.'

'Pray give it back. They're scarce.'

The doctor nodded and laughed. 'You shall have it,—and with interest. You suggest that Joe's passions and appetites would run to waste in London. Do you know what purpose your Art serves?'

'Tell me what purpose you think it serves.'

'Why, it's an "innocent diversion"—a kind of tea-fight-and-penny-readings business to keep the rich out of mischief. It persuades you to stay indoors and be a good boy, and not go running about in the streets, where the bad boys are. A nursemaid to the weak-souled, that's what Art is. A strong man like Joe Baker doesn't need it. He can take care of himself. But city folk are afraid of a real life like his: they're afraid of making beasts of themselves, with genuine passions and emotions. So they manufacture a set of sham ones—an artificial *safe* world—a *crèche* where they can't hurt themselves.'

With a smile, Lane Thomson turned to Hartmann. 'Ingenious, isn't it? But not flattering.'

'It's true,' Mitchell cried hotly. 'We haven't the pluck, that's the plain truth, to live a natural life; and we take to Art for very cowardice.'

Thomson asked, with the humble air of a learner, 'But—would you have us all go into the country and keep pigs?'

'They would pay the rent,' Mrs. Thomson murmured with down-dropped eyes: and Mitchell suddenly wondered if financial difficulties were added to her other troubles.

'We're not Irish,' Hartmann suggested.

Mitchell glanced at Thomson. 'No. An Englishman pays his own rent,—or should do.'

'Should, in fact, be his own pig?' Thomson said, smiling still, though with a watchful glance at the doctor.

Thomson would not accept his opinions, then? None the less, Mitchell revelled in them. The genuine—not the artistic—emotions were for his money, henceforward. And an earlier theory, once talked over with Hartmann, availed for loosening the bondage of old prejudice. To be one's self; to let one's instincts go free that they might struggle for existence, and the fittest of them survive,—this had always seemed logical to him; and now, in doing that, he saw the joy of adventure, the glory of daring where others were timid. So the old guidance was recklessly discarded.

Fortunately, another took its place. Not only

was the change in his mental habit justified and applauded by these views, but in their light he saw something ridiculous in his former fastidiousness about marriage. . . . Union of 'soul'? What did that mean, but agreement in those fashionable tastes he was learning to despise? For any reasonable man, clean physical union and the wholesome physical emotions should suffice. About Miss Sanderson he did not know much, but he could see that she would be an affectionate wife, and he was sure that she would be true. Those steady, pale eyes—when they wakened beside him in the morning, what better could a husband desire? . . . The doctor loved now to see a man with his arm around a girl's waist. It assisted his imagination of his own encircling Edith.

And the desire of marriage thus encouraged, he gave himself up to all sorts of pleasant day-dreams connected with it. Looking round his bachelor room, it was pleasing to think what an agreeable change in it a wife might make. Mrs. Clarke's care achieved only cleanliness and order: it failed wholly to give the touch of imaginative affection that he was aware of in the homes of married men. His rooms seemed hard and indifferent to him, almost as if in a hotel. A wife would change all that; and why should the wife not be Edith Sanderson? It was most illogical to expect to love her intensely, until marriage had made them perfectly intimate. And even more absurd was that poetical fiction, so long adhered to, that somewhere was one woman purposely fashioned by Providence with a view to her being his perfectly adapted mate.

XIV

It was towards the end of June that an urgent letter reached Mrs. Clarke, calling her to Rothwell to her old brother Peter, who, Doctor Wright thought, could not last many days. But Wright did not know what his patient was made of; and Mrs. Clarke found her brother sitting in his chair by the fire, almost as well as he had been six months before. Out of doors was the odour of pinks and of honeysuckle; within, the cottage smelt sweet and crisp from the turf burning on the hearth. A monthly rose swayed at the window; and looking at it, and to a distant stretch of woody hill, the old lady sighed. 'I shall be glad when we gits back home again,' she said, dropping instinctively into her native patois.

'Ah . . . I wouldn't live in London, not for a fortune.' The old man chuckled, as though his life were still to spend.

'Be ye sure of comin' back wi' the doctor at all?' asked old Peter's daughter-in-law, in her high-pitched voice. She was a woman Mrs. Clarke never much liked.

'What d' ye mean? Why not?'

'Well, we 'ave 'eard . . .'

The old man interrupted. 'Doctor Mitchell 'd never cast off Sairy. She no call to fear about that.'

'What have ye heard?' his sister asked, as coldly as she could.

'Oh,—nothin' but tales, Sairy. *I* don't set much by 'em.'

'They may be true, all the one for that,' the young

woman snapped. 'They says as 'ow Doctor Mitchell's gwine to get married. An' then he won't want you, ye know ... I dunno' what you'd do. You might come 'ere, on'y there's grandfather....' She looked doubtfully at old Peter, as though reckoning whether he would live until his sister needed a refuge.

'You needn't trouble 'bout me, Maria, not afore I asks ye. I dessay Doctor Mitchell 'd provide for me.'

'Sure he would,' the old man muttered. Yet his sister was evidently uneasy. She had to muster all her calmness to say, 'But who is it, then? *I* 'ent heard nothing.'

'Oh, 'ent ye? We've heard as there's some young woman—what was her name, gran'father? Thomson? was that it? Miss Thomson?'

'Oh,—I reckon you means the young lady what's a-living at Mr. Thomson's. Her name's Sanderson. If so be as it's she, I couldn't wish for nothin' better.'

'No, 'tent she. They said as 'ow Mr.—Mr. 'Ardman was after she,—an' like enough to git her, too.'

'Well, ther' 'ent no Miss Thomson; so we no call to believe it.' But poor Mrs. Clarke was sadly alarmed, for all that. 'Who told ye?' she asked. 'Somebody as knows more 'n their betters, *I'll* be bound.'

'No; it come round to us from Joe Baker, what's keepin' company with young Fanny Mansell up there. Oh, there's something in it. But I never heerd the name.'

Old Peter mumbled feebly, 'Well, if she's as good a one as Mrs. Wright, she'll do. I should be glad for 'n to bring 'ome a wife like she. We misses 'n,

Sairy. Tell 'n that. Doctor Wright's very good, but 'e don't onderstand our ways same as Doctor Mitchell do. He don't come an' sit an' talk our talk an' make 'isself one *of* us, ye know.' The old man maundered on cheerfully, until Mrs. Clarke had to leave. Then very quietly, as she kissed his forehead, ' Dessay I shall never see ye agen, Sairy.'

' We'll hope for the best, Peter.'

' It's as the Lord wills, Sairy. He'll 'elp ye to do without me, when I'm gone.'

Seeing that Peter had been largely dependent on his sister, his faith seemed likely to be justified.

When Mrs. Clarke returned to London, there was trouble between her and the servant, whom she accused of gossiping. That young lady took the first opportunity of calling on her friend Fanny at Lane Thomson's, to give her a piece of her mind. As it chanced that they were alone in the house, the talk was loud with excitement; so that Miss Sanderson, blessed with a latch-key and returning, quite needlessly, 'to see about Mr. Hartmann's tea,' could not help but hear more than she wished, before reaching the kitchen door. ' I shall tell Joe what I likes,' Fanny was saying. ' Besides, I never told 'n all. He kep' on ast'n whose photo 'twas in the drawer. He held me in the corner an' said he'd kiss me ontil I did tell. But I never told 'n. Besides, Missus shouldn't 've give 'n her photo. . . .'

Edith's unlooked for appearance cut short the talk at this point; but she had heard enough to cause her some distress. The hint of wholesale kissing, too, displeased her, and she shuddered daintily, remembering that Mitchell had recently professed approval of unrestraint such as this. Truly, he was a very savage, untrimmed kind of creature himself.

Yet, could she but have known, for something like three weeks the savage, untrimmed creature had timidly hesitated to ask her if she loved him. It was absurd to hesitate, of course. But he had hardly seen her without her aunt, and in fact had not quite made up his mind. In the presence of the two of them, his feeling was not of the kind she would spontaneously return. Singularly enough, it had too much of the old romantic reverence for womanhood to be practical. If somewhere in walking he could but take her arm, and press it—and teach her through her senses and blood, perhaps then she would respond. But in the meantime, he was thinking a good deal of Mrs. Thomson's hint of money troubles, and dwelling rather greedily upon impossible schemes for helping her out of his own abundance.

Hartmann, sounded on the subject, privately asked Edith, who, after speaking confidentially to her aunt, told Hartmann with a laugh, 'Auntie says you and I are her two pigs who pay the rent.' The blush that followed delighted Hartmann; but Mitchell, although informed that he had no need to worry, remained dissatisfied. 'It isn't fair,' he grumbled to Hartmann. 'You and Edith double her work. They only keep one servant. And yet Thomson goes buying bric-a-brac. I wanted to smash that vase he was purring about to-day.'

Hartmann shrugged his shoulders. 'I daresay he makes four or five hundred a year on his newspapers.'

'And spends it all. Damn him!'

In fact, the doctor's latest theories, which were

driving him fast by now, had little respect for Thomson's household gods. News from Rothwell, of Mrs. Wright's safe delivery of a daughter, on the other hand, delighted him. It was the consummation of his two friends' perfection in his eyes: 'a bit of real life,' which alas! contrasted sadly with the futility of Mrs. Thomson's existence, viewed from his standpoint. She was merely wasting her life,—and not happily. A pressing invitation to her from the Wrights, to come and see the baby, was the occasion of another of her outbursts of nervous excitement. 'I shan't go,' she said contemptuously: 'Fred doesn't wish it.... Oh no, he hasn't forbidden it. He simply takes no interest. And then, *I* lose interest in everything.' If a man had spoken so petulantly, Mitchell would have laughed; but the low voice-tones were so full of the feminine, that his senses were touched as by the very throat itself that spoke. Yet her glance forbade him to reply; and next day, when he would have forced the subject forward, she checkmated him with the most courteously-mannered of snubs. 'My dear doctor, you mean well, I suppose. But it is so ridiculous to hear you scolding Fred. You'll never know him that way. He's got any amount of good qualities that you have never suspected. And if he *has* a few trifling faults,—why, is it fair to keep looking at them? When I see them, I don't want you to whip him.' And again: 'I know you think I'm wasting my life.... But what else could I do, so good as helping Fred? Oh, I know your theories; but I don't care a pin for them. And I wish you didn't. I hate theories. All I want is to be more worthy of my good husband.'

This was undoubtedly better than her irritable and despondent mood, yet for a normal state this was not good. The inexplicable notion of being 'more worthy' should not have occurred to her at all; but apparently it seldom left her, even in her gayest moods. Mitchell, knowing well how great the strain on her nerves must be, used all his powers to persuade her to neglect her 'duties,' and to take up some diversion, artistic or otherwise. She turned upon him his own arguments used towards her husband, and with a laugh accused him of two-facedness. 'One man's meat'—he began—'is his wife's poison,' she said quickly. 'No, doctor, one artist in the house is enough. . . . I'm going to cook the dinner.'

But one hot night, towards the end of June, by ten o'clock Mitchell was yawning for bed. He was lonely and cross, swearing at all concerts in general, and especially at that one to which Thomson had dragged his wife with Edith and Hartmann. They had laughed at his ill-tempered refusal to go with them, and especially when, called 'a Philistine,' he had assented, 'Yes; thank God, I am!' He could see that Mrs. Thomson didn't want to go; and now it irked him to have missed the chance—small, indeed, since Hartmann was there—of coming home with Edith.

Suddenly, roused by the ringing of his bell, he stood up, and Hartmann hurried into the room.

Hartmann was paler even than usual, his dark eyes dancing excitedly, and his speech impeded by an angry stutter. 'Mrs. Thomson . . . I've just brought her home in a hansom. She nearly fainted in the hall, and doesn't get round quite well.' Excitement made his Cockney accent conspicuous.

In a minute they were in the street; Hartmann still stammering with anger, Mitchell soon perceived. 'I believe you're right, Mitchell, about Thomson. Would you credit it, that man was going to let her come home alone. She told him not to come—you know her self-sacrificing way,—damned folly, I call it!—and he said, "Take a hansom, then. . . ." So I jumped up and insisted on coming. Edith wanted to come too—she's a good little girl—but he said *no*; she mustn't miss that music. . . . I've had a lively journey, I can tell you. She's been half-fainting at times, and scolding me in between for coming, though I had to hold her up when she got out at last.'

A twinge of envy shot through Mitchell, to be driven out at once by anger. He didn't even swear; all he said was, 'I shall tell that man what I think of him to-night. I could see she wasn't fit to go.' Hartmann exulted at his cold, determined tones.

But there was in store for Mitchell a new and very unwelcome experience.

The servant was bidden to say that Mrs. Thomson had gone to bed, and was feeling better now. But the doctor was asked to go up. As he mounted the stairs behind the maid, the polished balustrade, the tasteful wall-paper, and all the bric-a-brac, glittering and yet shadowy from the hall-lamp, disgusted him with their air of unfeeling correctness. Superficial, imposing, unhomely, sedate—these things were insincere eyes of propriety, flattering to their owner, but supercilious to the bitter-hearted Philistine who passed them in the dim lamp-light. And the neat-figured girl, preceding him noiselessly, might have been the minister of some sombre enchantment, so heartless was it all to his senses.

But, with a quiet 'This way, sir,' she ushered him into Mrs. Thomson's bedroom, and—and there it was otherwise. Of details he noted nothing. It was her own room, without a trace in it of her husband's more restless and virile tastes. The lamp over the mirror was shaded to a quiet orange tint, harmonious with the gold and russet that relieved the creamy hangings of the bed and window, and with the soft fragrance, almost imperceptible, that freshened the pleasant air. Mitchell's eye fell on his patient, whose brown hair, looped up, lay dark on the pillow; and as her cool-voiced greeting reached him, he had to clench his teeth and pull himself together, thinking, 'This won't do for a doctor!' His knees were shaking, and a delirious, drunken sensation was choking his throat and lungs. It was gone ere he had sat down by the bedside; but only to return the more fiercely when he saw the bright hair quiver at the woman's temples, and the arm and hand steal out from under the coverlet. His hand on her pulse shook as it had shaken once before ('*Lucky dog*,' Hartmann had said, hearing of that occasion); and now . . .

Her voice calmed him: 'I'm afraid Mr. Hartmann has alarmed you, doctor. But I'm not ill.'

'No; you're not ill. You'll be yourself again in the morning. . . . I was only'—he gave a deprecatory laugh before adding,—'savage, I think.'

'It was too bad to bother you so late.'

'Oh,—you don't suppose I minded coming! It was the—the occasion that upset me.'

Then her voice was hurried, almost whispering, so that he had to bend closer to hear, because the servant was waiting at the door. 'No, no, doctor.' He noticed that her eyes shone appealingly. '*Don't* blame Fred. It hurts me; and it was my fault that he didn't come. Poor old Fred! He'll be so vexed when he gets home and finds me here.'

Mitchell was silent; knowing better than to contradict her just then. She went on: 'Promise me now, that you'll not be angry with him.'

The promise was given; needlessly for that night, as it chanced. Edith and her uncle had not returned when Mitchell left. But in the darkness of the street his anger grew hot again. The hair, the pale face on the pillow, the wrist he had touched, the lips that spoke so deliciously, the warm breath,—what was Thomson's so great worth, that he dared neglect all this treasure, which it was his privilege to spend all his life for, if he cared—his duty, whether he cared or no? Mitchell walked for an hour; and at home again, took the photograph from the drawer. But it was quickly replaced; the remembered face on the pillow was so much better than that.

They were troublous times for Mitchell. In the morning, black and heavy shame descended upon him. Emotion such as he had felt in Mrs. Thomson's room—quite new to him too—was such as no doctor has any right to experience. He foresaw that, if that was to be the rule, or even a frequent occurrence with him, it would be better to give up his profession, which truly, of late, had in other ways afforded him far too little of its old satisfaction. Were he only married, all would be well; but the hope of that wore no bright colours on this dismal morning. He had made no advance with Edith; and it was displeasing to remember that she had been a party to her uncle's unkindness last night.

It followed that his call upon Mrs. Thomson was made in no generous humour. Lane Thomson had waited an hour before going to his work, expressly to see Mitchell; who, mindful of his promise to the wife, yet could not forbear a rather sneering retort to the question, 'What do you think of her?'

'What she chiefly needs is a little reasonable care.'

Mitchell was not pleasant to look at when his eyes blazed. But the other met the gaze unswervingly. So with looks they struggled, and the doctor, hampered by his promise, knew himself beaten. Then Thomson gravely shook his head: 'We're not built alike, Mitchell. I can see you think me very wrong. . . . But that is not to the point. What do you advise me to do with Nan?'

'That depends on how she is.'

'She's better. . . . *Well*, she says. But I told her to lie still until you came.'

'Then—you'd better send her away to Rothwell for three weeks.'

'She told me last night that you advised it. But she doesn't wish it. I can't persuade her; but if you can . . .'

'I'll see. . . . Wait until I come down.'

The doctor felt quite self-controlled and businesslike this morning; perhaps, as he hoped was the case, because Edith's presence in the room was affecting him. He wasted little time in formalities, but began almost at once, with a brusque cheerfulness: 'Yes, you're better; *but*—you must obey my orders now. . . .'

'Well?' There was a gentle laugh.

'And start next Monday to Rothwell, for a month's rest.'

'Oh—but . . .'

'Excuse me; am I the doctor, or are you?'

'Edith—Edith! help me.' Her voice was comically pathetic.

Mitchell turned. 'Edith'—he had never before used her Christian name to her, and to his joy she flushed—'get pen and ink and paper: and an envelope and a stamp.'

'They are here, Doctor Mitchell,' the girl answered a little chillingly.

He continued, laughing the while at Mrs. Thomson, who was biting her lip and shaking her head to Edith. 'And now, sit down and write that your aunt hasn't been very well, and is coming . . .'

'No, no; I'll not be forced away like this.'

'Have you got that, Edith? . . . is coming, for a month . . .'

'Not a month. I *can't* go for a month.'

'Three weeks, then,—not a day less. . . . You can finish it, Edith.'

Mrs. Thomson put her hand out, and took his. 'Now, *please*, doctor . . . please! Let me off. . . .'

'I intend to wait here until the letter is finished, and post it myself. Let me see, Edith.' The letter was silently handed to him, and, having read, he handed it back.

'Mayn't I even see?' The tears were coming into her eyes; and more gently he replied—

'Of course, if you like. Now, don't be silly. Lie here until lunch. . . .'

'Oh, but, if I'm going away, I must be busy preparing. I must get up at once.' The other arm came out from the coverlet.

'Well—if you like. . . . I'll get out of the way first.'

That awkward last word annoyed him. Edith certainly flushed; and her aunt, whose face was turned from the light, said rather hurriedly, 'Yes—you deserve a scolding, doctor! You'd better hurry.'

When he was gone: 'I feel rather carried away, Edith,' she said ruefully.

The girl's lip curled delicately. 'Why did you let him do it?' she asked.

'Why,' was the quick and watchful rejoinder, 'did you obey him and write the letter?'

For answer her niece blushed fiercely. Then, 'I *hate* it,' she said.

At that a glad light came into Mrs. Thomson's eyes. 'Somewhen you'll be glad of a man's strong will, when you haven't one of your own, Edith.'

Mitchell, exhilarated by his success, had left Thomson with a jest, 'Now you'll know what a bachelor's life is, my friend.' But, as he posted the letter, remorse almost as sweet as his exultation came over him. 'I'm afraid I bullied her rather badly,' he murmured; 'I wonder what Edith thinks of it.'

Certainly, he found it not unpleasant to remember how submissive the lady had been.

XV

ONE July afternoon—it was the second day of Mrs. Thomson's being with the Wrights—the two women had taken wicker chairs on to the lawn, which sloped gently in the sunshine down towards the brilliant garden. The heat that was quivering dazzlingly over the whole valley was tempered for them into the quieter warmth of shade from laurels at their side, surrounding a great airy acacia in which the bees hummed perpetually above them. In similar shade, away across the valley, could be seen two or three cows clustered peacefully in their upland meadow, their tiny size emphasising the spaciousness of the hollow brimming with summer air, in which swallows sped arrowy, or floated as on a sunny sea. Now and again a swallow would twitter; and there was still the monotonous murmur of insects' wings; otherwise, no sound broke the silence of the vast sunshine pouring steadily down. Instinctively the two friends gave themselves up to the splendid calm of the afternoon. To speak was to risk breaking the charm of it.

Yet presently the baby, that had been sleeping on Mrs. Wright's breast, stirred, and the mother-talk began—the babble that only a mother can talk perfectly and without shamefacedness—and the great summer-day in its comparative insignificance was forgotten, was left to take care of itself, as it so well can. The two women bent fondly over the child.

At the same time, in the shady open doorway under the vine-clad verandah of the house, Doctor

Wright appeared. For a minute he stood looking at the two bent heads, the dark-brown and the fair, pictured against the deep green, and the long blue line of hills in the dreamy distance. It was a beautiful bit of glowing colour to watch. As he stepped out into the heat, the women's heads slightly turned, but no word was spoken; and silently he reached their chairs, and bent his head between the two to look at the baby. Even his discretion the mother would not leave unwarned: the quiet of her face said 'hush,' although she did not look up at him. But against the infant lips he had caught sight of his wife's breast, just showing between the white folds of her dress. 'Be careful: you mustn't take cold,' he murmured, leaning now with one arm rested on the back of each chair. In the same quiet tone, his wife said, 'It is safe on such an afternoon as this.' Very gently she half turned towards him, and leaned back into the angle of the chair, smiling at him.

His left hand was against Mrs. Thomson's shoulder. Presently she too turned, and putting up her own right hand, took his and held it lightly. The wife smiled approval to her husband. For a minute, while the bees' humming was heard, they were very still: then Mrs. Thomson, her fingers twitching ever so little, said very quietly, 'It is so good to be here.' She glanced round, and again away at the hills, to add, almost inaudibly, 'You don't know what you're doing for me, having me here.'

'Of course,' said Wright, with a still laugh, '*we*'re not getting any pleasure from it, *are* we, Emily?'

Mrs. Thomson saw the wife's answering smile,

and again her fingers closed gratefully on her friend's.

Through the burning daylight, dyed in the shade there, with blue reflections from the deep sky, the slight colour on her face and neck bloomed like ripening fruit; and, looking at her, Wright said, 'She looks better already, doesn't she, Emily?'

The mother rocked gently with her baby, and said very softly, 'We owe it all to Doctor Mitchell.' The baby was clasped closer to her as she spoke. 'All, and more,' she added.

Dreamily Mrs. Thomson said, 'I must write and thank him for making me come.' She released Wright's hand, continuing, happily: 'But I am very lazy. I haven't even given his messages in the village yet.' She nestled more easily into her chair, smiling to Mrs. Wright, who said, 'There is plenty of time.'

'Come with me presently,' Wright said. 'I must go into the village again.'

His wife looked up. He leaned over and kissed her forehead. 'If you'll come too, we'll go at once. I'm afraid of your catching cold here.' He reached down, to take the baby; but seeing Mrs. Thomson's hands eager for it, yielded to her, while the mother stood up, fastening her dress. 'Mitchell ought to be here,' they said, as they went indoors.

. . . . .

In that first week, Mrs. Thomson learned that she had never before known anything about the meaning of summer. It had none of the gay, light-hearted, frolicsome character, none of the spangled, fashionable eighteenth century lightness—that is the best we can remember of it o' winter nights. Each morning when she rose, she found the day already solemn with calm heat. The silent hills, whose colour changed always from silver-grey to steely-blue as the day wore on, lay sleeping, prostrate in the immensity of the light. Then, as she rode with Doctor Wright on his rounds, between gorgeous hedgerows or high up in the daylight on the open downs, the inconceivable miles of splendid summer wherever she looked took possession of her fancy, until, again halting at the gate of some cottage-garden aflame with roses, she was recalled to the miraculous details of the whole; to the thick-crowded vitality, all drinking-in the sunshine, absorbing it moment by moment. She was very silent during those drives; and her companion, watching the flush of interest on her face, where the sun-burn was steadily mellowing, forbore to interrupt her.

Now and again, a sense of terrible relentlessness in the unclouded deeps of the sky caused her a shuddering of the spirit. For Wright's face was sometimes grave when he came out from some cottage and told her of the slackening of the springs for want of rain; or of the poverty already feared if the drought should continue and work be interrupted. Yet, not realising that sorrow, she gave her delight wholly to the inanimate world's deep enjoyment, and her eyes to its intense splendour of colouring. Who that knew these daring contrasts, these magnificent burning harmonies, would give another thought to the paleness or to the enfeebled gaudiness of pictures hung on a wall?

And during that first week, her life at Rothwell

was a mirror of those great peaceful days. Her leisure seemed endless as the sunshine, yet as full as was the sunshine of delicious and manifold interest. In the dreaming quiet of her room at night, sleepy with the intoxicating hours out of doors, she could not remember how the day had gone, yet knew that there had been no time for her letter of thanks to Mitchell. 'I must do it to-morrow,' she said to herself each night.

And one morning she did get so far as to call on old Peter, to know if he had any message for his sister or for Doctor Mitchell.

She found the old man leaning over his pig-sty. He straightened up to touch his hat and answer her 'Good-morning,' then steadying himself against the sty went on in a homely, quavering voice: 'Yes, 'tis rare weather for we old 'uns to crawl about in. I bin a-lookin' at my pig. He's the last 'n o' my own I shall ever see, an' 'e ain't doin' very well. I've fatted a smart many in my time, but I be got too old now. Must leave it to the young folks after this. I be purty nigh done for.'

She tried to divert his thoughts, admiring the vegetable marrow growing in almost tropical luxuriance from the noisome outlet of the pig-sty, the little sheltered garden sloping up towards a fir plantation on the brow, and the glimpse of sleeping hill seen far beyond the valley in which the village nestled below them. 'Yes,' the old man said; ''tis a rare country. I ought to know. Eight-and-seventy year I've lived here; I be the oldest in'abitant; and now 'tis my time to go. . . . No; I ben't cast down about it. I've done my bit, same's the rest that's come an' gone. We ben't wanted after a bit, that's the truth o' the matter: we ben't *wanted*.' His voice grew cheerful with animated satisfaction. 'There ain't none o' the old 'uns left now, what I knowed when I was a boy; but I never seen the summer come round without 'ay-makin' an' harvest. Same's I said to my sister, we be sent 'ere for a little while, and then another generation is sent: but the Lord, 'e bides always.'

Was the old man going to *cant*? Mrs. Thomson looked away at the distant immemorial fields, and at the village; all as they had been for so many, many years. 'Eternal summer.' Who had used that phrase? She looked at the old man; then suddenly thinking, 'it was Doctor Mitchell,' she remembered her errand.

'No. I en't got no message as I knows of. I should like to a' seen 'n agen. Never was a better friend to we poor folk than Doctor Mitchell. But same's he said, when the bad weather comes and I can't git about, it'll be the last o' me. "You'll never git Peter to keep 'is bed," he says, "not ontil you nails 'n into 't." An' that's true.' The old man laughed. Then his face brightened. 'Tell 'n I hopes he'll be 'appy with 'is wife.' Mrs. Thomson started. 'Eh, ain't you heerd on't? P'raps I never ought to a' spoke, but we did hear as he was keepin' company wi' some young lady. . . .'

'Who was she? What was her name?'

'I thinks 'twas Thomson. . . . But now I minds me that Sairy said there wasn't no Miss Thomson; so . . .'

'Was it *Sanderson*?'

'P'raps that was it. . . . I can't say. My memory ain't what it was at one time. But if you ain't heerd of it, maybe it'd be best not to say nothin' about it.'

Here was news indeed! It was carried home eagerly along the sunny lane, and discussed with equal eagerness all that afternoon under the deep shade of the acacia. Why had Edith not told them? How had these people learned? No doubt the servants had seen and talked, before yet anything was settled. And 'Thomson.' They laughed; for this was almost as good as if Edith *had* been Mrs. Thomson's sister, with her own name. She was almost as dear as a sister; more dear, even, inasmuch as she was something like a daughter too.

Yet old Peter's message could not be sent. It would be unwise to hurry such a matter. Mrs. Thomson took a lesson from the summer's calm contentment. She would wait, or only mysteriously hint at what she knew; and must let her excitement cool down before writing at all.

With this added joy, the week passed. Then half another, still cloudless and parching; while the generous influences of the long days enriched her blood, her eyes were dazed with excess of light, and her fancy was steeped in sweet and gracious peace. After old Peter's talk, too, not only this one summer, but the old forgotten Julys, far back to the embalmed sweetness of Elizabethan days, added their fragrance as of old roses to her imagination; until, on her second Sunday, she knew that her life had never before afforded her so great a bliss as on that day.

For having spent within-doors a morning to which,

by contrast, the outer glare and heat gave a cool, white delicacy as of old china, they were sitting after dinner was over on the lawn again, and watching the almost imperceptible progress of the stately afternoon. The swallows had withdrawn to other valleys where water was more plentiful, and gradually the talk of the three friends died away as though they were overawed by the full majesty of the summer. Everything was perfectly still; the only sound was the humming undertone of bees, and that was so solemn that it seemed like the silence grown audible. Far off, the blue hills slept; soft blue smoke stole up from the village below them, hidden by trees; the trees were motionless; and from the lawn they sat on, to the farthest hillside and away beyond—where the sea must be sparkling—the golden, burning sunlight lay as if entranced. But it was no trance—that tremendous calm: it was rather the silence of breathless worship—the world's kneeling reverence for the sun at his work. Every vibrating ray in those wide miles of glowing light was bringing life down; and every leaf, every blade of grass on the farthest upland, was as if tense with the passion of existence. . . .

Yes; the world was very good to live in. Had not those three friends their part in the sunshine, their share in the universal worship? They were here together, in perfect peace, and that was enough. Presently, as the old villager had said, they would not be wanted; but the summer would continue—the village smoke would still go up, the life go on,—the 'Eternal Summer,'—'the Lord,' as old Peter had preferred to say.

Mrs. Thomson watched, until the strain grew unbearable, then glanced aside at her friends.

Wright, with his pipe in his mouth, had fallen asleep on the lawn. Well, he had gained other peace, by that morning's work faithfully done.... His wife, regardless of the summer, was watching her baby's face. Yet she looked up and met her friend's glance with a smile, which caused the other woman a gush of tender consciousness that here she was at home. Then satisfying, passionate love seemed to take possession of the sunlit valley, and to mellow all the air.

To be called to tea was almost a relief; and when they went out again in the cooling evening, everything was softened, sweetened, with more of fairness and less of awe.... In two directions, a long way off, the evening church-bells were ringing. They took the fancy travelling outwards, away and away under the golden sky, and showed it villages and towns glittering in the level sunbeams, with the people restfully wending through field or quiet street, to enjoy the summer, or to worship old Peter's 'Lord.' Again the words 'we're not wanted' came with the sustaining feeling of something continuous; something to which one's self belongs, as a blade of grass belongs to a meadow. And with the feeling went strange, glad security, the joy of sympathy with something more enduring than one's self.

Naturally, Mrs. Thomson went to bed that night quite weary. It had been a day rich with continuous emotion as with sunshine; emotion so clear and harmonious as to seem like delicious rest, but emotion none the less, and such as cannot be endured for long.

XVI

THE reaction set in on the very next morning. There were no letters for her; and although she knew that her husband hated writing letters, it was hard not to feel a little aggrieved, for she had had but four in all, two from him and two from Edith. That Edith had not written was yet more disappointing, when such great news from her was hoped for. But Mrs. Thomson felt that she herself had been remiss in writing; and after breakfast she sat down dutifully to make amends. The task, however, was not an exhilarating one; for what had she to say? Nothing had happened; she had only *felt* deliciously. But if she wrote about her fancies, Fred would laugh and call her sentimental; something witty and clever was what he would prefer. She gave him that, in the shape of a humorous scolding, which left her dry and cynical for the letter to Edith. To her there were several domestic matters to be spoken of; and they also were an irritation, a waste of time, when the sun was shining.

Next day the hoped-for letters arrived, and were worse than nothing. Two hurried scrawls—that was all. The niece's was opened first. Edith merely said that she had no time. They were doing well enough at home. She feared the house was getting untidy; but she had been busy practising for a concert, for which she must go and make herself ready without writing more now. A postscript added: 'Uncle has a slight cold; 'but he and Mr. Hartmann are going to the concert with me.' Not a word of

Mitchell? How was it that he was not to be of the party?

Thomson's letter was absurd. It mentioned casually that Mitchell seemed to be busy; they had not seen much of him for some days. Then came a suggestion that old-fashioned furniture could sometimes be picked up for a song in country cottages; and directions followed to buy any that seemed worthy.... As if Mrs. Thomson would insult her friends and Mitchell's by bargaining with them for their tables and chairs!—and in this weather too. The letter ended abruptly, with the same excuse as Edith had made. And they didn't say they missed her, or wanted her home,—unless it was to tidy up the house for them! She handed the letters, one to each of her friends, and went out into the garden.

But when Wright came, asking her to share his drive, the kindness of these two went home to her, suggesting that it was unfair to be cross in their happy home. During the drive Wright's cheerful, serious talk—he told her of his old student days with Mitchell—brought the unspoken gratitude choking into her throat. In response, to please him with appreciation of his old friend, she told him of Mitchell's talk about the summer, and of the exaltation it had led her to on the Sunday just passed. At the end, 'It was a kind of religious feeling,' she said. 'But I can't regain it since.'

Her companion mused awhile; then, 'Mitchell has told me something like that. And he too loses sight of it, for months at a time.... I'm so glad you two understand one another. Next to my wife, I think I love him best in the world....'

I

She only said, 'He deserves it. I will try to write to him to-night. I long to hear that it's settled between him and Edith.'

* * * * *

On their return, Mrs. Wright made an opportunity to see her husband alone in his room. She shut the door cautiously; then turned to ask, 'How is she now?'

'All right, I think. She seems quite cheerful.'

'She's very brave, but...' Mrs. Wright sat down on the table, and tapping the floor angrily with one foot, continued: 'I wish we could warn that man—Fred.... This sort of thing will kill her in the long-run.'

'Hm!... You know, he's all right, really. He doesn't know she's worrying.'

'Blind man!' said the wife scornfully.

'I suppose he's the last she'll allow to see how she feels. Or else he'd do *anything*—he's awfully fond of her....'

As Mrs. Wright looked sceptical, her husband took her two hands, saying, with laughing admiration of her uncompromising attitude, ''*Tis* so, really, dear!'

The answer was petulant. 'Then he should show it. A woman likes to be told—likes to feel that her husband is in love with her still.... O you silly old chap!' She wriggled and choked and broke away from the husband's practical assent to her proposition....

At lunch Mrs. Thomson's cheerfulness, although rather quiet, confirmed the truth of Wright's report of her—or seemed to him to do so. But in the long afternoon, before he joined them on the lawn, his wife, cuddling the baby and endlessly studying its face as she softly hummed and rocked it, yet kept a furtive watch on her friend. And as she watched she sat sorrowing, waiting patiently to give the encouragement which, as she saw, would be required. Gradually even her humming ceased; and at last a sigh caused Mrs. Thomson to turn and say, with a wistful smile: 'It's *too* bad of me to let my bad temper make you unhappy.'

'Are you bad-tempered, dear?'

As Mrs. Thomson didn't answer, but leaned over the child so as to hide her own face, the other said quickly: 'Will you take her for a minute, while I go to see what Willie's doing?'

The baby wailed at the change, and before they had soothed it Wright came out. Mrs. Thomson's smile to him was reassuring; yet the wife gravely refused the kiss he would have given, saying by a look, 'Not before our friend here.' And Mrs. Thomson, swiftly observing, broke off her cooing to the baby, for fear that it should turn to a sob.

With ready intuition of the situation, Wright began to talk. 'Have you been looking at the fire over yonder? I've noticed the smoke all the afternoon.'

'Where?' They had not seen it, although one of them at least had been gazing straight at it for an hour. Great rolling clouds of smoke, amber and pearly grey, were drifting slowly along the ridge of the distant hill. 'A big heath fire,' Wright said; 'I should like to be near it. The people go, I'm told, by the score, to beat the fire out with sticks. I can fancy them shouting, and the fire crackling.'

'And I had thought the afternoon so peaceful—*here*,' Mrs. Thomson said sorrowfully. And, indeed, ten intervening miles of calm sunlight had shed their silent peace over that distant confusion and terror.

Mrs. Wright shuddered. 'We found some little burnt bones—a rabbit's, Willie said—one day on one of those burnt commons. I hate to think of it.'

An expression of horror escaped Mrs. Thomson. 'And I had been fancying that there was tragedy and—and unhappiness, only in towns. . . . With my eyes on this all the time.'

Again at tea she had the satisfaction of seeing that Doctor Wright was deceived by her show of cheerfulness. But she was glad to hear that he had a consultation that evening, in the town down in the valley on the other side of the hill. The wife's eyes she avoided, for they looked too searching; and after tea, to avoid them yet longer, she stood at the window watching those smoke-clouds turn rusty yellow and creamy white in the evening sunshine, while the clear, cool daylight that was reflected into the room seemed to bring with it a great stillness from the pale, far-off blue of the southern sky. In the stillness, as if perfectly belonging to it, she heard the mother busy with her baby; undressing it, kissing it in the cradle; then, as though herself were another child to be cared for, she felt her friend's hand on her shoulder, and her breath on her cheek.

'Would you like to stroll out?' Mrs. Wright asked.

'Yes.' Her hand was taken and pressed. She moved to the cradle, kissed the baby, and bent over it so long that the other came up wondering. Great tears were beginning to fall on the little bed-clothes. The long restraint was over then, at last?

Not yet. She stood up, tightening her lips and drawing in her breath. 'Yes, let's go out,' she said.

They went out into the garden; and without hats, for the great heat of the day was over. And neither spoke, until they had strolled into a secluded path, overarched by young trees. Then Mrs. Wright put her arm softly over the other's shoulders. 'Tell me all about it, dear,' she said.

The touch was enough. Mrs. Thomson turned, gripped her friend's arms, and laid her face on the young mother's breast. Then the tears flowed fast and unchecked; and Mrs. Wright, holding her, felt herself shaken by her friend's passionate sobs.

For many minutes they stood so: until at length the hidden face turned, and only one side of it lay on Mrs. Wright's bosom. The other cheek was flushed and stained; the eyelids were lowered; the lips smiled piteously. 'I am ashamed of myself, Emily,' the voice faltered; but with the effort of speaking the sobs recommenced.

With one hand Mrs. Wright began to put back and smooth the wavy brown hair from her friend's forehead. 'Don't hurry, dear; take your own time.'

Presently they began again, strolling up and down the path. Mrs. Thomson took the arm that was round her, and drew it closer; and then, 'It was your arm on my shoulders that did it, dear. . . . If Fred would only sometimes . . . or if he would let me. . . .'

'But he loves you, dear.'

'I believe it ... only ... I get to *feel* as indifferent as he seems. ... I've been so wicked to-day. ... That letter ... I felt as if I *hated* him.'

'Don't you know ...'—'how near that is to love?' she would have added; but the other interrupted passionately—

'Don't tell me I love him, Emily. ... I would be killed for him—I would do *any*thing. Mr. Hartmann thinks I'm wasting my life for him. I could love to do it, if only ... but now it's only *duty*. It's only pride. It isn't because I love him. ... Just one moment of sentiment, now and then, would ... Oh, but I've been hateful to-day. ... It made me writhe to see you and Willie so happy. And when you wouldn't let him kiss you this afternoon, I hated myself for being in the way. ... But I was jealous of the baby when you held it; I've been jealous of Doctor Mitchell, because your husband loved him. ... And then—and then—no, don't stop me! let me tell you now! I felt as if I couldn't live in London another year without—without ... and so I've been calling you and Willie selfish for talking of buying a practice in the country. ...'

Mrs. Wright shook her head. She could not trust herself to speak; and the low, self-accusing voice went on: 'No, dear. ... You've got your little one to think of before me. It's I that am selfish; and I deserve to be left to work this out for myself. ... And when Doctor Mitchell comes back here. ... There again I am selfish. You know how I've been wanting him to have Edith? Their children would seem more like *my* children. ... Is that unkind to *your* little one?... Well, I've wanted to throw them together. But to-day I've been thinking—What if they married and then they ... didn't care for one another?... You shake your head; but you don't know. Doctor Mitchell is altered, somehow. Sometimes I've been almost afraid of him; he looks—hungry-eyed, restless, unhappy. As if he couldn't trust himself. He might make a mistake. He never talks about the country now....'

'But that isn't your fault, dear.'

'Isn't it my fault, if, instead of making my home a pleasant resting-place for him, until—until he finds the woman good enough for him, I've made it wretched?... And I've done that ... I've made use of him. I've let him see me unhappy, and I'm sure he knows why it is. He thinks it's Fred's fault; and I can see they're bad friends.... O Emily! I feel as if I ought to go home and try to do better. And yet I'm afraid ...'

'Couldn't you ... explain it? Tell Fred?'

Mrs. Thomson laughed bitterly. 'Tell him what? Say "I'm doing my duty; but I don't love you? ... Besides—I'm not sure. The first day or two after I came here, I hoped—I thought ... No; it's no good, Emily.... Hark!' She stood listening. 'Wasn't that the baby?'

Mrs. Wright stood irresolute. The other said, more brightly: 'Let's go in now. You've done me good, dear. Shall we have some food and go to meet your husband?'

Over their light meal, at which Mrs. Wright made her take some wine, her wit returned in such curious pathetic fashion as almost to bring the tears to her friend's eyes. When they rose, and the latter asked, 'Do you still feel like going?'

'Yes,' she said, 'I'm braver now. . . . Dutch courage, I think.' But her shining eyes belied the swift bravery of her smile.

They went out into the luminous twilight that is the summer night in the country. In the hedgerows they could see the tall grass standing; the dog-roses swayed lightly, unfolded and sleepless. For in the far northern sky the glow of the sun lay, travelling solemnly, imperceptibly eastwards. And the white dusty road stretched away mysteriously; leading the fancy on over unseen countries all under the summer night.

At the ridge they stood listening. The street lights of the little town lay below them, but the silence that all day had slept in the blue distance had stolen over that and all the world. The faint, far-off barking of a dog produced a strange, lonely feeling. And now, a dull, monotonous murmur far up the valley grew suddenly louder; rattling and ever increasing, until the train that caused it drew up with a yelling whistle in the station a mile away. They watched it puffing away. . . . 'The last train up to London,' Mrs. Wright murmured, waiting in vain for its roar to die away. And Mrs. Thomson, listening to it mile after mile, fancied herself in it—wrenched her thoughts away, until she realised that following that receding roar were men and women with their own troubles, perhaps—breathing men and women warm to the touch, and ignorant of her as she was of them—and then drifted back in unconscious reverie to her own home: the London street, the lamp-lit dining-room, the stairs, her husband, Edith. . . . What were they doing? How should she find them when . . .

She started. 'Come,' Mrs. Wright was saying. 'I can hear Willie walking up the road.'

But so far off was he, that they had walked three or four minutes before they met.

And still subdued by that great silence, Mrs. Thomson, on reaching home, went soon to her room, and sat down to write her letter to Doctor Mitchell.

XVII

For the time being, Mitchell's unhappy scepticism as to the ultimate value of his work had resulted in a more careful performance of it. For, after all, it was only a private opinion of his own that the world would be the better if most of his patients should cease to encumber it with their unhealthy carcasses; and so long as, by the act of attending them, he bowed to their contradictory opinion, it seemed well to make his submission to it complete. His cynical or disinterested punctiliousness favoured a cool grasp of details by which he effected cures that would have enraptured him, had not his former personal sympathy and enthusiasm disappeared. But now his increasing skill and judgment were no real pleasure to him; they had in them too much of the diabolically clever for that. 'A damned work of art,' more than once he muttered on leaving some successfully treated case. 'I've made something out of nothing, and it'll never have any real vitality of its own.' 'Poor, patched-up things' he thought his patients, sneering at his own efforts at securing the 'survival of the unfit.'

Naturally, after days spent in this humour, he arrived home in the evenings weary and dispirited. The friends at whose houses he sought diversion, depressed by his listlessness, and generously attributing it to overwork, began urging him to take a rest. He half dreaded the idleness of a holiday, while mechanically turning his mind to the necessary preparations for it.

Meanwhile, the cruel, parching summer evenings had to be passed somehow. The London parks were a shabby annoyance to a man who knew what summer could be like out of London, and theatres had lost their fascination for him. By force of habit he went to Lane Thomson's, but Thomson without his wife seemed almost offensively cheerful in his insincerity or 'hypocrisy.' That was on the first evening. The next was devoted to music which Mitchell could not understand, and which consequently bored him. He supposed it clever, like his own work, and as far removed as that from anything really worth doing. As a last resource—for might not literature afford him some reasonable activity?—he turned to his long-neglected manuscript, once praised by Hartmann. It was a last resource, adopted after the failure of one or two attempts to break down the curious barrier between himself and Edith Sanderson. For her liveliness had cheered him, and her summer dress was balm to his tired spirit. His embarrassment had somehow quite recently disappeared; he looked at her cool, bare neck and it gave him a sense of restfulness. But when he proposed that they should all have an afternoon on the river at Richmond on the Sunday, she had an excuse at once: in fact, she preferred Sunday quietly at home. A suggestion that she should let him take her to a theatre met with a similar rebuff. Although hungry to be near her, his pride rebelled; he spent that evening, as well as the Sunday afternoon, doggedly writing, with such success as may be imagined from the kind of temper he was in.

Yet, whether she cared for him or not, the sight of Edith was a help to him, greater than he knew. Apart from her pretty face, she looked so thoroughly healthy. 'One of the *fit* to survive,' he would murmur, thinking of his eternal theories and the sickening difficulties they were occasioning him. 'The sort of girl who ought to marry and have a family.' None the less, being so ill at ease himself, her light-heartedness vexed him. In fact, with the instincts to which he was theoretically surrendering himself pulling at him fretfully in many ways at once, it was irritating to see her growing inexplicably happier day by day. Ought she not to have seen that he was unhappy?

Little as Mitchell suspected it, Thomson observed his uneasiness, and made a clumsy, masculine effort to divert him; remarking one day to Edith that 'poor old Mitchell seems out of sorts.'

'*Doesn't* he? His gloomy face makes me cross.'

'I'm sorry to see it. I think he misses your aunt almost as much as I do.' The big, shiny face smiled pleasantly. There had grown up an odd sympathy and confidence between these two.

'Am I not managing well enough, uncle?'

'Silly girl! As if I cared. It's good for your aunt, and there couldn't be a better substitute for her. She would ask Mitchell here and give him a jolly evening. Can you do that? And only have enough music to . . .'

'Of course, uncle. To deceive him, you mean. Yes; ask him. You'll laugh to see what a hypocrite I can be.' The girl flushed, anticipating fun and future praise from her uncle.

'Well, that sort of behaviour is the wisest.'

But Mitchell also could play the hypocrite; and forgetting his more personal difficulties, he gave at the supper-table an impression that he was enjoying himself. But he noticed several things meanwhile, and accounted for them either uncharitably or cynically.

His eyes were hungrily active; but what they showed him awakened in his other senses no sympathetic understanding. To him, it proved the domestic incompetence of an artist, when the gooseberry tart which Edith had made proved to be unsweetened, and there was only lump sugar in the house. Her uncle passed it off with a jest. 'He would have grumbled at his wife,' thought Mitchell, yet laughing too. And when Hartmann threatened the girl that he should complain of that pie to her aunt, and had his knuckles playfully rapped with a convenient spoon, Mitchell yet more densely said, 'Never mind, Hartmann, *I'll* tell her'; thinking all the time, 'If she knew, it'd spoil her holiday,' yet hoping to earn a rap on his own knuckles. The heaving of the soft folds of the blouse below the girl's throat, her flushed cheeks and shining eyes, and even her bubblingly excited laugh, failed to show him—what was very plain to the others—that she was nervously anxious that the supper for which she was responsible should be a success. After it was over, her uncle insisted on her sitting down. 'Don't tire yourself; we want some music presently,' he said; and he himself—an unexampled thing—superintended the bringing of the lamp and of the drinks. Hartmann ran an errand upstairs for the young hostess, who, in her white dress sat curled up in the sofa corner, laughing while Mitchell, at her side, bantered the other two on their usefulness. Near his knee, her slipper and an inch of brown stocking rocked gently. Hartmann, bringing the music she had asked for, actually stood with his own knee touching it. Mitchell, looking up to see her anger, saw . . . certainly not anger in her glance. . . .

And why need Hartmann, turning her pages for her at the piano, bend so closely to her shoulder as if he were short-sighted? Without looking at him, she smiled, with delicately flushed cheeks. The music, evidently, was not everything to them. Could it, Mitchell wondered, be really anything to any one—this seemingly frivolous chaos of skilful haste? Somebody's *Carnival*, she called it, while her uncle laughed joyfully; a jigging infidel preparation for an infidel Lenten Fast. Yes; not for that solitude Mitchell was enduring; that midnight desolation under cruel stars, amidst wild beasts or taunting fiends. And he had to wear the mask of enjoyment.

He walked home, angrily striking the echoing

pavement with his stick. The hard pavement, the blackness hovering between the brutal-looking street-lamps—these seemed fitter companions than those he had just left. He thought of Edith's foot; it had once made him think of marrying her! . . . 'The little empty-headed flirt,' he muttered, calling the pavement's attention to his sentence on her with a vicious blow. And her uncle—the fool—was flirting with his own niece!

He had not noticed the tranquil summer night high overhead, in whose peacefulness lay sleeping his own quiet village and the friends there, and starlit villages far away by the sea. To that he was as insensible as to the kindly human felicity, the enveloping social cordiality from which he had just come away.

XVIII

ON the Saturday evening of that week, Hartmann and Edith Sanderson, having the house to themselves, came to a great resolution. In the joy of it, the man would have forgotten his supper, but, as if anticipating her future duties, the girl insisted on feasting him; and at the end—they were momently expecting her uncle to arrive — they held one another's hands, while she said—

'Then *you* will tell uncle?'

'Yes. But not to-night. To-morrow, perhaps. Let's have our secret all to ourselves for a little while. He'll be tired to-night, and tell me not to be sentimental.'

'Oh, but, Ernest, this is different. . . . And—I

may scold you now, mayn't I? . . . I think you're wrong about uncle,—as wrong as Dr. Mitchell. He's really kind . . . and . . . and tender.' (Her own eyes had tenderness and to spare.) 'I *love* him. . . .'

'What?—Dr. Mitchell?' Her laughing lover's arms smothered her.

'Silly! . . . No, dear; I'm serious about uncle. . . . And I've longed so to help him . . . to help Auntie Annie. . . .'

She hesitated, with tears that were an unneeded provocation for another embrace; during which Hartmann murmured, 'I understand, dear. . . .'

'And now that we're so happy . . . you've made me so happy . . .' she was continuing, when Thomson's key clicking in the street door interrupted them.

It was long after midnight; and Hartmann waited only for an ordinary 'Good-night' to Thomson. And the latter, who had been out to dinner and was returning tired and bored, soon sent Edith off to bed. He was feeling unaccountably dismal, and wished to be alone.

The night was intolerably hot. He lay restlessly awake, longing for his wife. Something had reminded him of how she used to look at him, years ago. . . . Why not now? Then, sighing, he put away his fit of sentiment, and regretted having driven home from a hot room in evening dress and in a hansom.

At breakfast he saw in Edith's eyes what had reminded him of his wife. Had he not been a fool in shutting off sentiment from his own life? At any rate, these two should have their romance to themselves, to enjoy so long as the delusion lasted.

Pleading that he felt 'seedy,' he asked Hartmann to take his place with Edith for their customary Sunday morning stroll; and Hartmann consented.

After lunch Thomson was drowsy; he withdrew to his own room, and had tea sent up to him. There Mitchell found him, lying at length, and dozing over a Sunday paper.

'Done up?' the doctor asked laconically.

Thomson admitted that the heat was overpowering. He thought he had a slight cold.

'Want any of my help?'

'No. I shall have a Turkish to-morrow. . . . I suppose you're off for a constitutional?'

Mitchell shrugged his shoulders. 'What can one do? I shall ask Hartmann to come with me.'

'I don't think you'll get him,' Thomson laughed. 'He's otherwise engaged.' He nodded meaningly to the other's questioning look, but added, as Mitchell left, 'They haven't *told* me; I only surmise.'

Edith, who had been at the piano, had turned to show Hartmann her hands. 'Look,' she said, 'they're getting *so* stiff.' Hartmann took them, kissed them, and held them while she went on: 'That comes of housework. . . . I shall expect, sir, in my own house to have servants to do everything for me. . . .' She stopped abruptly, and, snatching away her hands, turned with a quick blush as Mitchell entered. 'I was just showing Mr. Hartmann my hands,' she explained hurriedly; 'they feel so . . .'

Mitchell had seen the fondness swimming in her eyes, and resented it. He took her offered hand, and, looking at it critically, asked, 'How do they feel, Hartmann?'

Edith's eyes flashed. 'They tingle! Doctor Mitchell,' she said, in a voice that tingled too.

Mitchell coolly looked round for a chair; but the chairs were covered with piles of music, and he remained standing, and looking down at Edith. Disregarding Hartmann's observation that it was awfully hot, he said, eyeing the girl's white and slender wrist, 'The best thing for hands and arms is work. Notice your servant's. . . . But I suppose yours are fit for all you want to do with them?' Then, as if she were an insignificant child: 'I'm in a bad temper, Hartmann, and want a jaw with you. Will you come for a stroll?'

'No; it's too hot. Go and smoke it off alone, old man.'

'Oh, if you like! Good-bye, Miss Sanderson.'

The front door slammed behind him.

Edith bit her lip, but Hartmann burst out laughing. 'What a big hump the poor beggar's got!'

The girl pouted, saying, 'He's a perfect bear. . . . Why doesn't he *marry* a servant, if . . .' She flushed; and Hartmann, putting his hands behind her waist (for they had stood up when Mitchell left), drew her towards him, and would have kissed her. But she withdrew herself. 'No, Ernest, you haven't told uncle yet . . . and—and Doctor Mitchell has disgusted me.'

'You mustn't mind him. . . . Certainly, he's behaved like a pig; but something's getting at him. Perhaps he'd have told me, if . . .'

'Oh, I'm glad you didn't go with him. . . . I don't trust him.'

'I like his recommending work to you. It's awfully good.'

'Did you *see* how he looked at the litter on the chairs?'

'I saw. . . . He's in a fine old muddle in his own house. Did I ever tell you of his manuscripts, all mixed up in a drawer with bunches of violets and other trophies,—a certain lady's photograph among them?'

'What! *Whose* photograph?'

'Oh, I oughtn't to talk of it. I wasn't meant to see. . . .'

'Oh, but it's *horrid*! . . . No; don't touch me! . . . I *knew* there was something wrong about him. I could *see* it in his face.' Her own face was white with indignation. 'I'll never speak to him again,' she said vehemently.

And since she and Hartmann were henceforth to have no secrets from one another, she told him of the conversation that she had overheard between the two servants: then of Mitchell's masterful behaviour, and her aunt's weak submissiveness, in the bedroom that morning. The thought of her own weakness on that occasion was loathsome to her. And then— it was disgusting to think of—but had not Mitchell skilfully contrived to be alone with Mrs. Thomson when they were returning from the Spencers? and was not his abominable melancholy coincident with Mrs. Thomson's departure? The evidence from numberless trivial incidents had a cumulative weight: the inference was inevitable. Both Thomson and his wife were to blame, if also to be pitied: the lovers agreed exactly in their apportionment of pity and blame, weighing the situation from the sweet-aired heights of sunny felicity on which their own life was henceforth to bask. And Hartmann, remembering that he had once in jest assured Mitchell that the kindest behaviour to Mrs. Thomson would be to run away with her, confessed that sin also to his shuddering sweetheart, and had tearful forgiveness.

'I didn't believe in wickedness then,' he said.

'That was because you didn't know Good,' she said reverently, kissing him on the shirt-front.

XIX

THE hitherto innocent but unhappy object of their suspicion, having reached them, as he said, in a bad temper with himself, had left with his anger turned against them. He had not ceased to wonder how he could ever have thought of marrying 'a little fool' like Edith Sanderson; yet the loss of that hope had left him face to face with a distracting need for some other share in the world's progression —a need no longer satisfied by the work which now looked to him so often like a sham. 'A black-coated and respected impostor — am I?' he was continually asking himself, hunted by a constant unfaced fear that the true answer was *Yes*. That was the question he intended to put to Hartmann; and instead of putting it, he had been almost requested to take his departure. 'If *she'd* been at home . . .' he murmured to himself. . . . 'She understood, that night. . . . "We must stick to it, my friend." . . . Why must we,—if my case is as hopeless as hers?'

Her sluggish husband with the newspaper suddenly returned to the doctor's memory.

'Yes; her case is hopeless. Why, I can't even talk to him about *mine*—a much more logical affair. . . . I'd as soon talk to Jack there. . . . Yes, Jack. Oh, she's wasting. . . . And I'm wasting. . . . If it wasn't for her—I believe I'm a help to her—I'd not stay in London another month. . . . I wonder what Wright 'd say, if I never came back from my holiday?'

He strolled on, sometimes talking fitfully to the little dog that was wagging along beside him. 'No, Jack, I can't tell Wright. I don't want to make him as miserable as I am. But he'd never understand. He'd think me mad, old dog. . . . Or else I'd run down next Sunday. . . . By Jove! *She'd* be there, Jack! And we might get a talk. Eh, Jack? Might I give her your love? It would do me good to see her. She's brave,—and in a harder place than mine. No way out of it for her—unless . . .'

He had reached the park where he and Hartmann had walked some weeks earlier. Again the amorous courting couples were there, and while his mind was preoccupied, his senses were observing them. Could he—the question kept recurring with a sugary allurement—have the impudence to go down to Rothwell next Sunday, if Mrs. Thomson should still be there? 'For, oh! I *want* her—want her help and pluck,' something within him cried. Why not? Thomson might smile—his fastidious, oily, superior smile—but he wouldn't object. And who cared if he did? . . . And that pair of ninnies. . . . 'I'd throttle Hartmann if he dared look at me.'

Mitchell's hand closed across the hooked handle of his stick, and the fibres snapped.

At that he lifted his head as a man awaking from sleep, and seeing an empty seat, dropped into it. The dog bounded up beside him.

'I'm a strong man, Jack, and a bit of a savage too. Let's think about my holiday—where to go.' But instead of thinking, he watched the people idling by in the warm, summer evening air: gaily dressed girls and their sweethearts; or quieter-looking matrons with their husbands and children in fantastic Sunday clothes. . . . 'The people I'm wasting my life on,' he sneered. On the next seat to his sat a man with his arm round a girl's neck, oblivious of publicity. Mitchell choked down his momentary feeling of disgust. 'It's *genuine*, at any rate. The courting's well enough, Jack; but the married life!' Hartmann's probable future was imagined. 'Slippers and piano-playing. It's too pitifully small, even for those two small souls.'

But what could Mitchell do better, if he were married? *If* . . . 'How if I went abroad, Jack, in my holidays, and never came back? Eh? . . .' And he went on, to himself: 'We'd live fast; no sticking about in slippers with nothing to do. No rotten piano-playing and domestic parties.' His fancy pictured hurrying adventures, fierce excitement, and giddy whirling pleasures, dangers shared with his wife, and strange infinite knowledge acquired in outlandish ways that left no opportunity for getting bored, and gave endless opportunity for bringing out the waste strength in himself, and for unfolding the latent splendour, the wit, the courage, the passionate love of—of a wife that didn't exist for him!

Suddenly he sat up. 'Jack . . . it's a bad business. I'm afraid I'm in love. Let's go home.'

Feeling strangely tired on his way, he took a cab. His arrival in that unaccustomed manner alarmed Mrs. Clarke, just home from church, and exhibiting quiet religious peace in her best black clothes and all her bearing. The thin old face looked anxious, and the aged voice was tremulous as she asked, 'I hope there's nothing the matter, sir?'

'Only laziness,' he laughed; but added, in the solitude of his own room, 'Poor old soul! What the deuce should I do with her, if . . .' The 'if' meant so much, that he dared not even to himself complete the sentence.

After an absent-minded supper, he sat long into the night; forgetting to smoke, but thinking—endlessly thinking. When at last he stood up from his chair, he went to the drawer in his writing-table, and, taking out the photograph of Mrs. Thomson, examined it hungrily. 'She's better than that; infinitely better. . . . But that throat is glorious. . . . Oh, I love her—body and soul! . . . And *now* what am I going to do?'

XX

THE first thing to do was to get some wholesome sleep, if that should be anyhow possible, in order to obtain guidance from the unsullied emotions of a quiet awakening. But sleep withheld itself from a mind wandering in greedy awe, as it were, through flame-lit, thronging gardens of pleasure, intoxicated by their ravishing possibilities, and yet as by some unseen monitor bidden to close the eyes, and refuse the unholy enchantment.

Yet, sleepless as Mitchell had lain, with the summer dawn came a kind of awakening. Into the sweet morning sky, how the larks must now be singing their way up, at home at Rothwell. Carters, through the dew, with blissful pipes smelling fragrant in the young morning, would be going now to the stables at all the old farmsteads. One or two of them must soon be passing by Mitchell's own garden. . . . They could be heard 'Nice mornin', Bill,' and so on, from the bedroom windows, if any one should chance to be awake there. . . . There might be some one, with brown hair looped up and deep eyes—some one whose husband talked of Art, and spent a stuffy Sunday afternoon over an ill-printed newspaper. And she was enslaved to him: shoe-black, and cook, and general drudge for him, yet striving to love him, while in her absence he fooled with his own niece.

Perhaps her attitude was very splendid; and Mitchell's own desires very shocking. But he had not slept. And the riotous visions of the darkness had provided him with weapons of their own against sentiment, and especially Christian sentiment. Wherefore the dawn's dewy suggestions were swept away as by a searching wind; he called them prejudices, the creations of timorous habit too long substituted for spontaneous impulse. Honour, chastity? Nature knows nothing of them; like discretion, they are the virtues of cowardice. Let a man know what he wants, and afterwards call it by whatever names he will!

Well, as yet he had not committed himself; and failing sleep, there was work to do, thank Heaven, for a diversion of his thoughts. It was intensely necessary to come to the subject fresh and sanely from the outside. For his was no sickly, dilettante, French amour, but passion mingled strangely with puzzling conceptions of duty—duty to himself, to the woman he loved, to society, to his profession. It involved the making or the marring of his whole life.

So all that day he fairly slaved at his work, calling on every patient whose condition afforded him the least excuse for coming again so soon. Yet, with all his vigilance over himself, again and again such thoughts as this escaped his control. 'Ah, my friend, you'll not see *me* many more times.' Then he made to himself the juggling excuse: 'Well, I'm going for a holiday, and perhaps shan't come back.'

In fact, although he did not see it, his old habit was making a last struggle for its mastery over him, against the theories which, if they displaced it, were to fling down the reins and flourish the whip over his passions.

But the strongest habit may succumb to sheer weariness of body and brain.

In such utter weariness, Mitchell's prejudices, still keeping guard over his 'Honour,' called for a truce that evening. There were four unoccupied hours to get through. How, after all, could he by himself determine anything? Let it stand over until the following Sunday; then, if she gave the slightest sign on seeing him—a blush, or a warm hand-pressure... Meanwhile, he would not look again at the photograph.

He had furnished himself with papers of the sort that Mrs. Clarke disliked; and he spent his evening turning them over, ashamed of their vulgarity. It clashed with delicate recollections haunting his mind in the benumbed state of his passion, until that passion derived from the contrast the justification of refinement; almost of altruism. Was there really anything in it to be ashamed of or to dread? One peep at the portrait—he allowed himself one at last—sent him to bed proud of loving such a woman; finally, hugging a wonder as to what had disturbed him so abominably all day, he easily slept; and slept so long that in the morning there was no time for reveries, in the hurry from bed to breakfast.

There was awaiting him an invitation from Mrs. Spencer, to meet Mr. Lane Thomson with his niece and Mr. Hartmann at dinner, Thursday evening. 'The very last people I want to see, as it happens,' commented Mitchell bitterly. Mrs. Spencer's note continued: 'I called there yesterday, supposing that Mrs. Thomson would be returned; but it seems that she may be away another fortnight yet, and by your advice. I hope you'll not have to attend poor Mr. Thomson. ("'Poor Mr. Thomson,' indeed!") He looks worried and out-of-sorts. Naturally, perhaps. At any rate, you must come and help us cheer him up.'

The note was torn up into small pieces. 'Well, she may as well get her hand in at pitying him, perhaps. I suppose he's been moaning to her.... And to think of such an old Pharisee being able to influence *Her*.... One of the she-dragons that guard the marriage-system. I should like to bid Hartmann beware . . .'

He was wrathful, recognising the exquisite torture the said she-dragons (of whom Edith Sanderson would eventually be one) are able to inflict on a true live woman. Had he not once been permitted to witness some of that suffering? . . . Would that that journey in the train could be repeated now! . . . He would be ready to soothe—was not she ready even then? She had seemed so touchingly submissive to his suggestions; just as, more recently, she had obeyed him in going away! True, she had protested that she, and he too, must fight out their own troubles. . . . But how, if that had been a challenge to him? A test of his courage; a touchstone of the genuineness of his modern theories about marriage, at which she had gone out of her way to scoff that evening!

If that were so, why had he not recognised it at the time? The answer was humiliating: it accused him of cowardice, of shirking the issues which fact was presenting to him. Recently he had told Thomson that Art was a mere toy to keep men out of mischief; but were not all his own pursuits—his profession included—cleverly calculated to the same end? A stupendous hypocrisy, in fact? The innocence of any joy began to look like *prima-facie* evidence of its insincerity. For years he had been skulking behind his duty as a physician—a veritable sham!—pleading it as an excuse for not following this or that impulse of which at heart he was afraid; and the cowardly habit had asserted itself that night in the train. He had been tried and found wanting.

By downright cowardice, he had chosen to save the lives of his miserable and disgusting patients, and to let drift all the vivid wealth of life,—the personal beauty, the brilliant wit, the tender, sensitive emotions, of the woman he loved, and who was calling for his help. He had been respectable! But now! He had done with all that now! He shut his teeth, but his lips curled grimly as he abandoned himself to frantic day-dreams of a careless, adventurous future.

In that mood his Tuesday was passed. Wednesday brought torturing doubts whether his reading of Mrs. Thomson's behaviour to him was the correct one. But on Thursday morning her letter came, and his doubts were removed.

She had sat in her room writing late, by the open window, so that the hushed charm of the summer night was upon her spirit still, stirring it as softly as the gentle night-breeze stirred her hair or swayed the flame of the two candles on her table. As she was beginning, a moth had flitted in and fallen singed upon her paper, and the tears had come into her eyes; for life just then was so real a thing to her: she and the moth, the train she had watched, and the faint mellow stars that flashed palely in the glimmering sky outside, all seemed only parts of something less fortuitous than individual life—more inevitable, more intensely living. And in this mood she had written:—

'MY DEAR FRIEND,—I will not ask your forgiveness for not writing to you sooner. I had thought each night to repay you with a letter, for having been wiser than I, and sent me here against my will.

The reward would be too pitifully small, even if that were all I owed you for. But it is for much more than sending me here, and giving up this lovely home to the friends I love—it's for more than all that I am your debtor.

'It never can be paid: I don't wish to pay it. I don't even think of *rewarding* you now, as I write. The reason for writing is a better one. It's because somehow,—here in your house (I have the room at the end, against the greenhouse. There is a rose looking in at the candle-light. And over beyond the village a night-jar is crooning—as if it were the summer night stealing through the trees)—here in your house, which seems like my real home, yourself are very real to me,—as if you were a brother. (How I wish you *were* a brother, or *some very near relation to me*!)' She had underlined the passage, thinking of Edith.

'Perhaps I had better begin with confession, or you may misunderstand. For this delicious holiday was to be your medicine, which I was as unwilling to take as a naughty child. I shall obey you gladly another time, for this *has* done me good. But you mustn't suppose I am cured. To-day has shown me that I am the same weak-minded, rebellious woman you sent away,—not really changed. I have behaved shamefully to-day—and to these two friends, who are goodness itself, of course. . . . I seemed to look ahead, and see the rest of my life—the same old round of "duties," all needless—a mere series of unsatisfying days, with now and again a holiday at Rothwell—just enough to keep me going. The only escape seemed to be if I could drown my consciousness of it in "pleasure." And that I despised. . . . Half my life seemed gone (I shall be thirty-two next month): and I saw myself growing old in a pitiful search for mere courage to keep on through the second half, when the first had been such a failure.

'That was this afternoon. Then Emily let me cry it all away on her bosom. . . . I suppose it was the revulsion from too great happiness, of which, perhaps, some day I may tell you; for it partly was connected with you. (Do you remember talking about the summer that lives always—in seeds, and in people's work, from one generation to another . . . ?) I had been full of hope; and it is coming back again now. This letter is helping it; I can't tell you how, and if I did, should hardly dare. Only, as I said, you seem so *real* to me to-night: everybody does. . . . I can fancy Edith; really drawing her breath at this moment,—can almost catch the pleasant odour of her dress-stuff (do you know it?) and the warmth of it. . . . And then I thought of you, and wanted to . . .

'I can't *say* what I mean. This letter must serve as a symbol for it. Perhaps you'll not understand. You don't *need* friends, as I do, to lean upon their strength. I hope you never will; but if you do— there are friends hungry to prove to you what they would never *say*; they will come, though, at a sign. . . .

'If you understand that, I don't care about anything else to-night. I have made myself quite tired. Ever so much about the Wrights and their baby must wait until I come home; and I'm growing restless to get back and try again, since there's no shirking.

At present I feel as if I shall do ever so well; yet you must be prepared to find me very cross and horrid, after I've been home a day or two. However, we shall see. . . . I am going to bed now. Good-night.'

. . . . .

As before Mitchell had despised his patients, so to-day he hated them for demanding his attention to their unhealthy bodies, when he wanted to be thinking of sweet breath (not Edith's) 'really being drawn at this moment, and the pleasant odour of dress-stuff, and the warmth of it,' where it may have touched the letter—'the symbol'—now warm again, in his own inner pocket. Besides, he longed for leisure to consider one uncomfortable question: 'What would Wright think' of what he was going to do? To that came this reply: 'Wright must know me as I am. I won't have even *his* love on false pretences. I won't buy friendship—no, nor even love itself—by *being* a coward and *seeming* a man.' So he shut and bolted behind him the last door by which he could have returned; and, in the name of Truth, set himself to ride rough-shod over the social virtues. And certainly some of the glory of martyrdom upheld him; his spirit would have fitted a persecuted Puritan, had its earnestness been on the opposite side. But, you see, the fact that there was a lady in the case, who was to be rescued from durance, made him rather a kind of knight-errant or cavalier battling for the other side of life. He did not suspect then that the two sides might be arcs of the same circle, and that there was a centre from which the two might be united.

He hastened home for a belated lunch, although

not hungry for that. Hardly could he wait for old Mrs. Clarke's withdrawal, to get up and find his treasures—the photograph and the bunch of withered violets, which had been at Mrs. Thomson's waist. With these beside him, and the morning's letter spread before his plate, he began his lunch.

Mrs. Clarke tapped and entered. She saw with what he was occupied, and could not speak for consternation.

'Well?' he said angrily, to cover his instinctive or habitual shame. He had never spoken to her so before.

Her answer had the coldness of affronted propriety —not undignified in its way: 'Miss Sanderson sent about an hour ago to say would you go round as soon as you can. Mr. Thomson is ill. . . .'

'The devil he is! . . . Very well, Mrs. Clarke. *You* needn't wait. I'll go, of course. . . .'

Alone again: 'Confound the old woman. I must pension her off, and the sooner she's out of the way the better,' he muttered. Then he forgot her, suddenly realising that probably he would not have to go to Rothwell next Sunday after all.

XXI

A PATIENT look of preparedness, such as Mitchell had not before observed in Edith Sanderson, reminded him suddenly of her aunt, and gave him an unintended gentleness, when, softly closing behind him Thomson's bedroom door, he found her waiting on the landing outside.

Leading the way downstairs, she asked him there, 'Is he very ill?'

'Not alarmingly—yet. . . . Pleurisy; and a touch of congestion.'

Thomson had in fact taken a severe chill, which he had severely neglected, having never before experienced anything like illness. He had not had his Turkish bath.

Mitchell directed Edith as to keeping up the temperature of the room, and the proper methods of poulticing. Seeing the girl's lips tremble, he added, 'You needn't be frightened, although he'll probably be much worse before he's better. I've told you all that can be done at present. By the way, of course you'll telegraph for Mrs. Thomson?'

'I have done that.'

Mitchell looked at his watch. 'She might come to-night by the last train. I'll meet it.'

Edith's head lifted, while her eyelids drooped guardedly, in her aunt's manner, as she looked up replying, with a kind of aggressive smile, 'You're very thoughtful; but Mr. Hartmann will do that, thanks.'

Somewhat astonished, Mitchell rejoined: 'It would be better for me to go. I could prepare her. . . .'

'What for? For something you haven't told me?' The girl's face grew pale; but still she gazed watchfully at his eyes.

'Oh no. Only . . . you see, Hartmann may be useful here.'

'Thanks; I'd rather he went.' She turned away.

'Why?' Mitchell persisted.

'I have my reasons.'

'Well—I'll look in again.' He departed, wrathful under this rebuff. 'You're pretty, my young lady,' he sneered to himself; 'but you'll never get your aunt's kind of beauty. If you weren't qualifying for one of the she-Pharisees that will hunt her, then perhaps . . .'

It might have profited the doctor to follow out this suggested reason for the distinction between beauty and prettiness; but he was too excited for such analytical business. He persuaded himself that nothing could have come of meeting Mrs. Thomson that evening; he had no plan. Meanwhile, who cared for a little girl like Miss Sanderson? Or what could she—what could any one do to obstruct him, now that Fate was working on his side? For, not as yet recognising the wish that was father to his thought, he was already picturing the woman he loved, as a widow, perplexed by business and tenderly appreciative of a man's support and help in it.

He passed a piece of public garden, where the afternoon sunlight seemed to insinuate itself lovingly, as if seeking coolness, under the parched leaves of the plane-trees. It reminded him of his own home —the country home Mrs. Thomson loved so well. First, with the Wrights, as his dear and honoured guest he would welcome her there—next spring, perhaps. And then—well, he could wait, since the Fates were taking the matter out of his hands.

Ah—but the irony of the situation!

On the pavement by the public garden he stood still; and gripping the railings, stared between them in abstracted thought, unconscious of exciting curiosity in the passers-by, until aroused by a boy's voice—

'Yew'll cop it, mister, if yew tries to git over them rylins!'

He walked on, soliloquising: 'My dear boy, those are not the railings I'm anxious to get over. I'll risk "copping it" for the garden I want. But suppose your life depended on their being down; you saw them falling, and then found that *you* were the very person expected to set them up again!'

For, indeed, Mrs. Thomson was not yet free: the railing wasn't down; Thomson might live; in all likelihood he *would* live, if Mitchell did his duty. The very man whom the Fates seemed to be favouring was to be head and chief of the resistance against them!

'I suppose I'm hoping he'll die!... Well, why not? Apart from me, it would be better for his wife; and no worse for any one else. What earthly use is such a fellow?'

Yet Mitchell went home, and carefully mixed the necessary medicine himself. And to Mrs. Clarke's anxious inquiries he replied that Mr. Thomson was decidedly bad, but he hoped to pull him through. His conscience was touched by the wistfulness of the old woman's expression, reminding him that he had behaved to her almost brutally an hour ago. But he could not stop to give heed to that.

Six o'clock.... She could not be home for four or five hours yet.... Four hours in which he had nothing to do. There were indeed some patients—not serious cases, but people whom he occasionally called on when he had time. There was no time this evening, though!

Then Jack came whining, anxious for a walk. His master looked down at him. 'No, Jack; not this evening. I can't think about going out now.'

Nothing to do; and yet no time.

For in truth, through the quiet, sunny evening, his desire was straining forward to the moment when he should meet the woman he loved. . . .

Meanwhile, black and panting, whirling through mile after mile of peaceful valley, through small stations in heedlessness of would-be passengers there, the train that was bringing her bore, if he had known it, a close resemblance to his own mood. How could he wait to attend to housekeeper, patients, or dog? What eyes had he for the calm, golden, evening sky? Headlong, hurtling thought was his, pouring itself recklessly forward upon that one moment, with rattling, fiery speed: hotter, darker, and more reckless-seeming as he grew closer to it—the fire being fed by exultant reading and re-reading of the letter—until in extravagant abandonment of all common-sense, he imagined his meeting with her; meeting of hands, of eyes, of lips. . . .

Ah! but—Edith Sanderson has spoilt his best chance of that. . . . Had she not better save her serious looks, for a while? . . .

Similarly restless, and heedless of the spacious evening peace through which the train crawled, Mrs. Thomson sat—a prey to horror and apprehension. She had no particulars; she knew only that her husband was ill, and that, if she had loved him as she ought, she would not have been so far away from him. Who could tell but that his illness was her fault, because she had not been in her place to take proper care of him? . . . He might be dying. . . . That dread crowded from her mind all other thought, except that the train was remorselessly slow and precious time was speeding away.

It was speeding there for her: it was dreadfully loitering with Edith, counting the minutes by her uncle's side. He lay in a kind of stupor, fitfully coughing at times; so long the time seemed that when he moaned and gave back to her his blood-stained, horrible handkerchief, she felt as though somehow the dragging minutes had slid back to the previous coughing, and were to be lived over again. After she had sent Hartmann to the station, the loneliness of her responsibility grew terrible; and there seemed something ominous in the ticking stillness of the house. . . . A candle was brought for her: she waited an hour. Surely they must soon come? . . . Then she started nervously; hearing a low knock at the street door.

It was only Mitchell after all: himself unable to wait. But at sight of him the girl's courage returned, and now she grew eager to get him out of the house again. Should he not wait with her? he asked. . . . Oh no; she could tell her aunt everything. Yet he lingered on and on: while each minute added to her dislike of the thought that he was only waiting to see Mrs. Thomson. . . . They sat long, saying nothing. At length she asked, 'Can you do any more for him to-night?' He feared not. 'Then I think . . . it's a pity for you to wait. I don't see why you should.' Her face flushed; her grey eyes flashed at him. Once more he had to own himself beaten, and he left, with all his baffled passion plotting to be even with this impertinent girl. . . .

XXII

AT her husband's door, that night, Mrs. Thomson paused a moment—it seemed as if her heart's beating and her whole life paused—in dread. Was she in time? For, as they were coming along in the hansom, Hartmann's assurances had satisfied her mind, but left her conscience unappeased. Then there came from within the room a low moan: her breath returned choking, and a fierce ache of remorse mingled with relief took possession of her, as she entered and Edith rose to greet her.

She took her niece's hands, and kissed her lips, but her eyes sought the bed always, and she whispered: 'How is he, by now?'

'No better; but dozing.'

The wife, slowly stripping off her gloves, stood by the bed and watched, panting, unconscious of anything but her suffering husband; until Hartmann, knocking softly, came in. 'Can I do anything?' he asked.

Edith shook her head; and to her aunt's 'Is everything here that he'll want?' whispered the few things that needed to be attended to in the night.

The patient stirred, and coughed, while they all waited, holding their breath at the horror of it. He opened his eyes, glanced vacantly at them without distinguishing his wife, and relapsed into uneasy stupor.

When it was over, Mrs. Thomson sat down in the chair Edith had left, and, clutching its arm tight, said, 'I suppose you've had your supper?'

'Edith ate nothing, though,' said Hartmann, in a reproachful tone.

'You must, Edith. . . . I? No; I can't. Has the doctor been again?'

'About twenty minutes ago.'

'Then—if you'll wait while I change my dress, I'll watch here. You two must go to bed.'

To exchange the dainty holiday costume for a useful, sober-coloured dress was an unspeakable relief, touching some hidden sense of fitness; perhaps the same sense that loathed the glass of wine and biscuit which, on returning, she found that Hartmann had fetched for her, and which she placed on one side, and shuddered at the sight of two or three times during the night.

She thanked him, but asked, 'Where is Edith?'

'She's . . . a little bit overcome. She began to cry when you went out,—hysterical, I think. She asked me to say good-night to you.'

'Has she gone to bed, then?'

'Yes. I made her take some wine first.' He hesitated, before adding: 'You look frightfully tired. Go and lie down for an hour or two . . . I'll call you if anything's wanted.'

She shook her head, and her eyes pleaded with him for that favour—to be allowed to spend the night by her husband's bedside.

And when Hartmann had withdrawn, she pushed aside her chair, and, kneeling by the bed, took within her fingers the feverish hand that lay near her on the coverlet, while she watched the painful breathing until her own kept time with it. 'My husband! my husband! if you'll only live . . .' In her mind the words were incessantly forming, and at that point breaking off into a sob that seemed to flood away all conscious thought. Once, to smooth his pillow, she stood up, and, although cramp seized her so that she almost fell when she stooped to kiss his forehead, she knelt again, disdaining the ease of a chair. So, sometimes moving to give him drink, but always sinking to her knees again, she spent the night at his side. It was, as it were, a feast of penitence, changing gradually, as the hours moved on, to something like reverence and calm. For a long time the sufferer lay still; she thought him sleeping, and her own thought wandered a little—strangely enough, from the candle-lit sick-room back to that Sunday afternoon at Rothwell, and its ecstasy of reverent worship for—she hardly knew what. Only she knew that now, somehow, the feeling was alive in her again. . . . Yet her gaze never left her husband's face; and presently he stirred, and opening his eyes, with a piteous attempt to smile, murmured, 'Nan. . . .' That was all. But the hot tears came: her fingers clutched convulsively upon his, and felt his feeble response. She bowed her head, passionately kissing his hand. 'My love! O my dear love! I will not let you die,' she whispered.

Against the bedside, she felt her heart beating strongly, and rejoiced because it beat for him. . . . Ah, yes! and so, through him, for all life—for the larger life of which he was only a part: the Power that, pulsing in her own heart and in his, and in whole generations of men and women, fashioned out of its own urgent vitality Religions, Arts—the Arts her husband loved—and beautified the hills and created towns and villages—the dear Rothwell village. . . .

. . . . .

The candle on the table beside her flickered. Surely it must be day? She rose and drew aside the curtains. . . . Yes; there was the sweet sunshine, high up in the blue. . . . And with the new daylight flooding into the room came daylight upon her new-born faith. For as again she knelt and kissed the hand she took, and again tried to feel the beating of her heart, she felt that not only living for love was excellent, but in working for it also there was sacredness. She smiled, detecting herself longing for that abhorred task of blacking her husband's boots; and then administered to her own mind a whispered forgiving reproof for the smile: 'May I not make, even of that, an act of worship?' . . . She kissed her husband's hand once more, and knelt on and on, until Edith came and prevailed upon her to go to her own room and try to sleep.

XXIII

HER thankfulness was too great to permit of sleep. With peace in her eyes, she rose again at her usual hour, and was able to receive Mrs. Spencer, who called very early to express her sorrow for the cause which had prevented her dinner-party from taking place on the previous evening. Her presence was endured because Fred would like it; but the trial was severe when Mitchell arrived and Mrs. Spencer still remained, talking, while the doctor went up to the sick-room alone.

Mitchell felt less resigned at the ruin of his hopes for this particular meeting. What encouragement could he carry away from it? Merely a warm handshake, that might mean only friendship; and a momentary faint flush, that might mean anything or nothing. There was, besides, a kindly inquiry as to his own health—a hint expressed that he was looking fatigued and worried. . . . Why, oh! why had he not made an opening for hinting in return that the thought of her was worrying him, that her tired smile, seeming to say 'You see, I've come back to slavery,' would drive him crazy?

Perhaps by such means she intended to compel him to rescue her; to kindle his pity until it should add courage to his hesitating love, and make him— poor coward!—speak? At any rate, the favouring Fates would demand co-operation from him; and he determined, accordingly, to lose no second opportunity. That very afternoon, perhaps, he might corner his lady; might awaken her blush to a brighter consciousness, and make his eyes and hers talk.

Yet, when in the afternoon he found her there watching her husband, her own grave anxiety took possession of him. He was disarmed by her very trust in him; and unexpectedly he was touched to sympathy with her distress, when he had to say that her husband was in serious danger.

Truly, her devotion to duty was admirable. What, then, would her devotion to love be worth? How beautiful for her to exercise, how mean to refuse her the opportunity!

Yes; but, blocking the way, now he perceived the greatest of all obstacles in her own sense of duty. To persuade her that the first duty was to herself—that might be the tremendous task before him, if Fred should recover. Mitchell sat down to consider that possibility. Were the Fates simply mocking him, making of Thomson's illness a means of tantalising him? Was the prize to be snatched away from him at the last—a sham of an opportunity? Or . . . good heavens! did the Fates that had made Thomson ill expect co-operation even to the extent of . . . !

He leapt up in terror, and rang for Mrs. Clarke, who found him at the window, gabbling to himself mere words without sense. 'Was there anything the matter?' she faltered, adding that she thought him looking unwell. He laughed. 'Did you ever know me unwell? No; I'm going out to dinner, Mrs. Clarke, and forgot to tell you before. I'm all right.'

And 'I'm all right. *I'm* all right!' he kept repeating in the street, as if to crowd out of his mind that thought which he had not dared to finish. And now, what could he do? or whither go with a certainty of finding talk for the evening—talk that would save him from that thought that was trembling like a poison-drop over the edge of his consciousness, momently threatening to fall into it?

Mrs. Spencer that morning had asked him to come over for the evening. He hastened now, as though the very air were crying murder in his ears; and he breathed freely only when the Spencers' door opened, and the old man's hand gripped him back to safety.

Often afterwards he thought of that evening: of the room's depressing hardness, which yet seemed so sane and tranquil; and of the elderly couple, so well-agreed in their torpid happiness.

From the good yet sober-looking furniture, propriety seemed to glare upon him watchfully as from Mrs. Spencer's spectacles. Everything was formal, respectable—as if the horse-hair chairs, long ago banished to the lumber-room, had left behind them a tradition of decorous hospitality. And Mitchell's nerves appreciated the staid, secure, comfortable domesticity, even while he contrasted it scornfully with the happiness he intended to win for himself.

Of course, they spoke much of the Thomson's; straying at last to 'poor Mr. Thomson's' views of life. At Mitchell's hot defence of those views where they told for loosening of the marriage ties, Mrs. Spencer gazed astonishment over her spectacles. Her fingers, busy over their knitting, grew still; and a glance at her husband showed him unobservant of their guest's excitement, but uncomfortably turning his glass round and round on the table.

'Wait until you're married yourself,' Mr. Spencer laughed tolerantly, desirous of changing the subject. But Mitchell's suggestion, that marriage seemed not to have affected Thomson's views, stirred Mrs. Spencer to the retort, made with a dreary head-shaking, that Thomson's own married life had been nearly ruined because of those views. They had alienated his young wife, so that she formed indiscreet friendships with other men. Mitchell's face burned. Was Mrs. Spencer talking at him, or was there any basis for her insinuations? 'We can trust you, Doctor Mitchell,' she said. A circumstantial story followed, consisting, however, chiefly of Mrs. Spencer's disapproval. Her husband, looking up at last, suggested mildly: 'But, you know, there was nothing wrong about it, my dear.'

Much relieved, their guest laughed excitedly. 'Merely Platonic friendship, Mrs. Spencer.' He drained his glass of whisky and water as though he would wash that conviction well into him. Spencer refilled the glass, while his wife shook her head again, saying: 'I don't believe in Platonic friendship, Doctor Mitchell.'

'But, surely!... You don't accuse Mrs. Thomson of... *She's* not *that* sort of woman!' Mitchell's face was white and angry.

The old man laughed nervously. "But your theories should approve such things, Mitchell.' And Mrs. Spencer grimly commented, 'Ah, Doctor Mitchell's heart is better than his head.'

He denied it; yet his head swam for a moment. The solid furniture seemed to swing round, mocking him; and another gulp at his glass was needed ere he could say hastily: 'I don't like to hear a lady's name...' The word failed him; and Spencer said suavely, 'Well, well, doctor, we're her friends. You needn't defend her here, to us.'

At Mitchell's dogged reply, 'I don't know,' Mrs. Spencer's knitting ceased again. She gave him one of her looks, asking, 'Has Mrs. Thomson made you her champion, Doctor Mitchell?'

The husband struck in hurriedly. 'No, no! I quite

understand him. You do right to take her part, Mitchell. But you needn't mind us. If my wife talks severely—why, she means no more harm by it than . . .'

'Than Doctor Mitchell by his theories,' Mrs. Spencer said, when her husband hesitated. She smiled over her spectacles, and insisted on Mitchell's once more refilling his glass; 'or I shall think you're offended. Let us talk of something else.'

Mitchell laughed. 'I think you'd better'; for the whisky was glowing in him, until he thought exultantly, 'They dare not talk—to me.'

At eleven o'clock he departed, inflated with a new-found confidence in himself. His arms tingled with inspiring strength. 'I'd take her to-night, if I were ready,' he thought; and, springing into a hansom, he found the joy of imagination even in his regret that Mrs. Thomson was not then beside him, speeding through gas-lit streets, eastwards, dockwards, towards the dark sea and their travels. . . . Never mind; he would drive his way through at last; reckless as this cabman, bribed to hurry. At Thomson's door, although he knocked softly, Mitchell felt victorious: he strode up the stairs masterfully—the owner, in his own belief, of the only treasure there.

Not a shred of pity did he feel, in the hushed and heated sick-room. A small and shaded lamp cast a stealthy glow over the room, showing dimly on either side of the bed Hartmann and Edith Sanderson listening awestruck to the sick man's delirious mutterings, as though to messages delivered from another world. The lamp was purring gently, in complacent derision of the room's solemn stillness. Mitchell heard it, with ironical approval, yet silently stood and watched too; the others glancing from him back to Thomson's flushed face, wondering what dreadful tale it would tell. At last the doctor turned away, beckoning Hartmann: but it was Edith Sanderson who followed him to the door. Her looks were beseeching, until he spoke.

'Is your aunt prepared?' he whispered.

What caused her to flush, and dart sudden anger from her eyes? 'Aren't you going to do anything for him, in this dreadful state?' she whispered pantingly.

He stared down at her in astonishment; then, coldly: 'There's no more I can do. Another day will settle it one way or the other. Good-night!'

Her lips trembled, but her eyes fell; and she made no answer, waiting for him to go. And, nodding to Hartmann, he went out, feeling that he had silenced her.

But when the door was shut upon him, she stamped her foot; and, returning to her place, whispered angrily, 'He's been drinking.'

Hartmann's angry look satisfied her; and she worshipped his self-control, when he said only, 'I'll tell your aunt to call in some one else to-morrow . . . if it's not too late.'

Still elated, Mitchell went out into the soft-carpeted passage. His eyes seized greedily on an upright streak of light, where a door stood ajar—a door he had once entered. And since his steps seemed inaudible, he realised that he must have been listened for, when the door opened a little, and Mrs. Thomson put her head forward, dark against the widened strip of yellow light behind, yet lit into dusky reality from the lamp on the stairs.

'They have sent me away,' she whispered. 'They said I must rest. . . . But it's too dreadful. . . . Tell me the truth, doctor.'

Her utter confidence in him touched him with shame at his recent brutality; and his eyes fell before the appeal shining in hers. He felt his face burn as he looked down, stammering, against his own will, and shocked at the falsehood: 'I—I hope . . . that is, I think . . . he may pull through.'

Then fierce desire caused him to look at her. Her eyes, full of suffering, pleading for the succour no man could give, shone upon him as if he were her only hope. She tried to speak, but he saw her lips tremble and go together again, in dumb anguish.

'I will do all I can,' he said softly.

There was a brave, grateful smile, and a glistening of tears in the shadow. 'I know it . . . I know it well. . . . But . . .'

Again his eyes fell. 'There is little we can do now,' he faltered, 'except hope; and,' he looked up persuasively, 'try to rest.'

She shook her head at that, and an idea came to him.

'Would it comfort you—I'd do *anything* to comfort you—if I stayed by him to-night?'

'Has it come to that? Do you think it needful?' she asked, apprehension growing in her eyes.

'I can't do more than—than any one else—for him. But if it would give you the smallest satisfaction. . . . You know, I'm yours . . .'

At that confession, desire tingled through him. But she, not knowing it, murmured gratefully: 'My friend! . . . no; I'll send for you gladly if there's the smallest change.'

Her breath came warm and pleasant to him, as she spoke. His eyes were devouring her face; and the massing of the dark hair, with the light shining through it from behind, suggested why the door was not opened. But in the moment while he paused, a murmur from her delirious husband reached them. She held her breath, listening with horror in her glance; then shut her eyelids, breathing painfully. For very pity, Mitchell could not keep her standing there. He shuddered in sympathy, and said, shaking his head: 'You really must try to rest. . . . And since you won't have me . . .' he held out his hand.

Her own was put to meet it round the door, the edge of which, catching at the loose woollen sleeve, drew it back from her fore-arm. How was it that he dared not observe that, but tried instead to direct his compassion into her eyes from his own?

The warm, drowsy-feeling softness of her fingers in his hand was a privilege; their grateful pressure against his own was the condescension of a saint to him, to be received reverently. He quickly loosened her hand, and whispering 'Now shut your door and lie down,' saw her kindly smile, heard the door shut to, ran down the stairs, and hastened out into the summer night. A deep peace came down on him: he hugged it, strolling for a whole hour in the dark streets, unconsciously enjoying also delicious respite from thought. For once, he felt, he would be able to sleep sound.

.   .   .   .   .

He had quite forgotten the unseen horror that had driven him to the Spencers'.

XXIV

FROM thoughts that looked like shipwreck Mitchell had been overjoyed to escape, that evening, swimming on a mood of calm; but next morning he found himself drifted back to his crazy craft of thought once more. For he was a man of theories at this period. By a theory, he had thrown overboard the charts as well as the mariner's compass of old habit, and was endeavouring, poor fellow, to steer by the tides! Meanwhile, circumstances had blown him hither and thither: he had drifted far, unconscious of drifting at all, until, as it chanced, a letter from Dr. Wright that morning caused him to open his eyes. Always, hitherto, one of Wright's letters had been eagerly seized upon: this one, to-day, was opened with regret, and caused uneasiness in the reading of it.

Evidently, Wright was unchanged; but somehow, Mitchell felt almost afraid of the strong, buoyant common-sense of the latter, because it indicated how unlikely was his friend to understand the change that had taken place. Wright had loved the Doctor Mitchell of former times: he might despise the present one: at any rate, he would never sympathise with him. How was that?

He wrote of one of those very problems vexing

Mitchell's soul—the doubt, namely, as to the ultimate serviceableness of a doctor's work. Mrs. Thomson, it seemed, had given the friends at Rothwell a hint of Mitchell's perplexity in this matter. 'By the way,' Mitchell thought, 'she must have understood me by sheer sympathy; for I've scarcely breathed of it to her.' That idea was to him a gleam of sunshine over his sea of troubles; in some roundabout way far more helpful to him than Wright's cheery conviction that the puzzle—which, said the writer, had troubled him also for two whole miserable days —would blow away if Mitchell, like a sensible man, came to Rothwell for a month's holiday with his old friend. They could talk the problem over, for fun, it was suggested.

Mitchell's uneasiness was great. He shrank from the whole proposal, and from all of its parts: to be a guest instead of master in his own house, an idler for a month among the village friends he had loved to work for—this was bad enough. And then, in his unsettled state of mind, he would prefer to avoid Wright; while, above all things, it seemed impossible to talk to him of his professional dilemma, when there was involved in it a far more important difficulty, of which he could not breathe a hint to any man.

This last consideration was the most distressing of all. The very first sight of Wright's unexpected letter was an unwelcome intrusion upon thoughts guiltily discordant with it, as though Wright had actually detected him in a dull regret that last night he had not kissed Mrs. Thomson's hand. He shouldn't care for Wright to know what he was thinking; and yet, that sort of thought must not be dismissed! Was it not a part of his theories that impulses should be obeyed, and thought, of all kinds, entertained? Dismissing the thoughts, would he not be a pitiful, hypocritical coward, posing as a man of courage and truth? Ay! and besides, there was Mrs. Thomson's welfare to consider!

So he pondered, on his way to visit Thomson, his mind tossing helplessly in view of two great problems: the chief one having reference to Mrs. Thomson; the other to the professional question to be discussed with Wright.

It is at such times that direction is given by the Mood. Not seeing Mrs. Thomson when he called, a wave of despondent feeling that she did not care for him cast him stranded on the other problem, as to the Good of Life, or rather, as to its Evil. He found abundance of pessimistic arguments with which to convince Wright, some day; and not one reason appeared on the other side. A pessimistic philosopher is dismal company, unless you can laugh at him. Hartmann, having taken holiday on that Saturday morning so that he might relieve his sweetheart and her aunt, saw Mitchell, and would have laughed at his lugubrious face, had not Thomson's grave condition banished levity from that house. For when all was said and done, Hartmann rather liked the doctor, and found it hard to believe that much was wrong in him. Of course he resented Mitchell's behaviour to Edith, and would take savage delight in telling him so; but he disliked extremely the task enjoined on him by Edith, of suggesting to Mrs. Thomson that Mitchell was not trustworthy as a doctor. Unluckily, however, before she went to lie down in her room, Edith had made him promise; and he attempted it accordingly, but in the unwilling manner of a man over a dubious-looking oyster.

'Would it gratify you, Mrs. Thomson,' he said when Mitchell had gone, 'to have further advice?'

She was leaning over her husband. Her startled glance upwards at Hartmann discomposed him. 'Did Doctor Mitchell propose it?' she asked hurriedly.

'No. But it occurred to me that . . .' He got no further in his sentence, seeing the crimson of reproach kindle in the lady's cheek. Beyond that she condescended no further in the way of a reply; but that was enough. Later in the day he explained to Edith that her aunt would evidently hear nothing against Doctor Mitchell.

The girl looked scandalised. 'You don't mean that she . . . ? Oh no, Ernest!' She reddened with the shame of her thought, adding despairingly: 'But I can't imagine what she's thinking of! I *must* warn her, somehow.'

Mitchell, in the meantime, finding a gloomy kind of security in his occupation of demolishing all conceivable excuses for preserving the lives of people better dead, was glueing his thoughts down to that subject, for fear of considering the other, which, perhaps, might settle itself comfortably for him in the course of the next few hours.

But hidden underneath his thought, there was unacknowledged thirst to see Mrs. Thomson again, and to touch her hand. Acutely, fretfully disappointed was he, therefore, at meeting only Edith, on visiting Thomson in the afternoon. Thomson was drowsing at last; uneasily, yet more hopefully.

'I'll prepare something that you must give him if he rouses up,' Mitchell said; telling the girl to send for it in about an hour's time. 'I think he may pull through now,' he added, leaving.

He truly thought so. So far, then, he had succeeded in destroying that chance of freedom for Mrs. Thomson which the Fates had almost promised. Not until now had he realised what Thomson's recovery involved. For himself the loss of the one woman in the world; loss of glorious love; condemnation to a hateful, barren, and lonely existence. And for her? Oh, worse still: discomfort, unhappiness, the degradation of living with a man unworthy of her, the waste of all her splendid life—one of the few lives worth saving, it seemed to Mitchell. And all this, merely because of keeping the breath in a heartless, faddling fellow whose sole reason for living was to write useless columns of trash for useless, trashy journals.

Not that Mitchell cared whether the man lived or died, if . . . if . . . if . . . He walked about his room, dwelling on that 'if,' the dog Jack watching him uneasily from the hearthrug.

By and by, he went to his writing-table, taking from the drawer the photograph, the two letters, and then the bunch of withered violets, tied with blue ribbon by her fingers. . . . What would he not give now, to have her once more breathing before him, placing them in his coat? Yet, when it really happened, how little he thought what it would come to in the end!

Now, as he thought of that night, there seemed something fateful about it; glorious, yet with a sinister touch too. There was a dark and dreadful feeling within him; a fancy of something horrible lurking round the corner of his brain,—surely he had half detected it once, like a drop of fatal poison? When?

He took up the photograph, and, kissing it, sat down, gloating over its beauty. As he sat, the dog came, putting its paws on his knees.

Mitchell stroked the shaggy head; and holding the picture for the dog to see, murmured thoughtfully: 'There, Jack! ... How shall you like her for your mistress, eh, old dog?' ...

Then, suddenly he put it down on the table, and began to walk about again. ... 'Mistress ... that's what they'll say. ... Yet what matters, if she's happy with me,—in Paris, or California—anywhere?' ... Still, the word galled him. He remembered Mrs. Spencer; her shocked talk, and his own scorn of her insinuations. And as his memory travelled back over that last evening, the fatal forgotten thought seemed to loom nearer, heavy with calamity. What was it? He could not remember; and presently was muttering: 'I must save her. Somehow I must save her,' over and over again. Anything; for the poison-drop of thought, baleful, was shuddering nearer and nearer to the edge of his consciousness. Not remembering what it was, he yet strove with himself to avoid it.

How was he going to get through the long evening before him? So much daylight there was yet to pass. The strong, late-afternoon shadow from his house as yet had hardly reached the houses opposite, aglow with sunshine. On their roofs, thick dust lay golden-brown against the cruel, wearisome blue, all smoke-wreathed. If one were out in the streets that careless, extravagant, yellow sunlight would shine all round one's thoughts, and mock them; it would reflect its iridescent colours into the brain's dark corners, as if into places where murdered men lay. . . . Mitchell turned uneasily from the window; paced his room again, studying the carpet, afraid to think of Thomson, yet aware all the time how the man's life hung on his judgment during the next twelve hours.

A shutting window across the road flashed a beam of light across the room. He shuddered; and finally, wondering painfully at his own nervousness, went moodily downstairs to the surgery, instinctively preferring, as if more in harmony with his mind and mood, the gloomy shelves of drug-bottles to the sight of the clear, hot, open air. He was alone there, the dispenser having gone to tea.

And there he had work to do, for a few minutes. He wrote out one or two prescriptions—Thomson's among them; and was about going once more upstairs, unwilling to see the dispenser, when the bell rang. He started nervously, then opened the door to Mrs. Thomson's pretty servant, who had come for the medicine.

'It isn't ready yet. . . . Can you wait?' he said. For some reason, he felt reluctant to prepare the mixture himself. But, as the girl hesitated, he said: 'Well, I'll put it up at once. No doubt you want to get back.' And reaching for a bottle, he muttered again: 'No doubt you want to get back.'

The servant sat down watching him, fascinated by

something that frightened her in his harassed-looking face and strange voice. He took a large glass in which to mingle the drugs; and she noticed that as he held it to the light, his hand trembled for a moment.

Then he seemed to stop and think, aghast; and again, in fierce hurry, to seize the next bottle from the shelf. What ailed him? What horrible thing could it be, like sudden poison pouring over his brain?

Dumb and motionless with terror, the girl saw his eyes suddenly grow startled, his lips part with a gasp, a spasm run through his arm uplifted for pouring.

At the same moment, the dispenser opened the street door. She turned, almost with a scream, and even as she looked away, there was a crash of glass on the floor, and a smothered cry from Mitchell—

'Good God! It would have killed him!'

The girl sprang up; and the dispenser rushed forward to Mitchell, who stood trembling. But the doctor put him back with a shaking hand, and shutting tight his eyes and teeth, and throwing back his head in a fierce effort to control himself, said at last, in a tone of dead constraint, 'I'm not well. There's the prescription. Make it up as soon as you can.' And so left, pale and tottering.

Not a word was spoken in the surgery. The dispenser's face was too grave for the girl to dare questioning him, even if she had had anything to say. But she longed only to get away; and once provided with what she came for, she hurried away as from a haunted house, out into the warm, companionable street.

XXV

Mrs. Clarke had been out shopping. Returning, she found letters in the letter-box, and, on her way upstairs, took them in and laid them on Mitchell's table, where she was horrified to see the photograph and Mrs. Thomson's letters spread out. As ill-luck would have it, she turned so hastily that her old black mantle flicked one of the letters on to the floor; and she was in the act of picking it up just as Mitchell staggered dizzily into the room from the surgery.

'Good God! what are you doing?' he asked, seeking to hide his own agitation and dismay under a cloak of bluster.

'I was only . . .' the old woman began timidly.

'Don't explain. . . . But I wish you wouldn't come prying into my affairs.' He tried to frown her into submission; but although her mouth twitched plaintively, the old truthful-looking eyes quelled him. Avoiding them, he flung himself into a chair, waiting for her to go.

'When would you like dinner, sir?'

'Not at all. . . . I want to be alone.'

She saw that his feet and hands were fidgeting with impatience. Stealing a glance at his haggard, frightened face, she left him, shaking her head ominously.

Alone at last, Mitchell locked his door. Then returning to the table, hastily he put up Mrs. Thomson's letters, turning away his eyes, lest by any chance he should see some unmerited word of friendship. 'I'm not fit to *touch* them,' he muttered. And again: 'Ach! . . . what a damned scoundrel I am!' as he put away the photograph, ashamed to look it in the face.

He sat down, staring blankly at nothing for many minutes. Then his wandering glance caught sight of his hand, grown pale with city life, and shaking now. A gentlemanly, respectable, murderer's hand. . . . And this was the hand that Wright would somewhen grasp, supposing it a true one. In abject scorn of it, he hid it. . . . 'A poisoner; a poisoner. . . .!'

The loathed flesh strove to make a kind of cringing defence, suggesting: 'But you had no thought of even trying to poison him. . . .' A defence drowned by overwhelming outcry from some other part of the man, asserting itself at last after so many days: 'You curséd, curséd, curséd blackguard! . . . You wanted the man out of the way, and hadn't even the courage of your own convictions!'

'But for Mrs. Thomson's sake,' the miserable flesh began, in the theoretical jargon of his last few weeks. Again it was interrupted from that other source. . . . 'You'd better leave Mrs. Thomson's name alone. . . . It was yourself,—your own foul, sneaking self you were thinking of all the time. . . .'

So, the husk or shell of Doctor Mitchell sitting motionless in the chair, the inward dialogue raged, accusing and accused; the accused still defending itself with all manner of theories, of deft logic and artful agnosticism, and still stamped out, choked, and flung back, as it were, scorched and wilted from the fiery accuser, regardless of theories, and scornful of logic and of all but its own burning light. The quick horror of that moment in the surgery, like flint meeting steel, had awakened, as it were by an electric shock, some dormant faculty in Mitchell, that now, arising uncontrollable and unexpected, was taking possession of the whole man; taking the guidance of him out of the hands of impertinent theory; with savage stripes scourging from pitiful brain and shrinking flesh all the soft, treacherous thoughts and desires so long harbouring in them.

They say that, when the warm blood begins to flow once more into a frost-bitten limb, the pain is horrible, unendurable. With a grind and a fiery smart and a wrenching ache of shame and remonstrance, it grinds its way, quickening the torpid nerves and senses to their duty. So, with unspeakable anguish, Mitchell's senses were quickened; forgotten faculties, or faculties he had never before believed in, began throbbing, and a terrified power of vision seemed to spring into sudden life. Not the vision of the eye,—*that* had disgraced itself, and was forbidden to exercise itself even in memory—but a vision which beheld the manifold desires and tendencies within himself. And from these, that inward eye shrank in horror; yet was unable to see aught else but the treacherous poisoner, or the cowardly, crawling dependant on Fate.

But, the process being beyond his experience, Mitchell was unaware of new guidance implied in it. As yet he saw only that the old was completely broken down—untrustworthy; a broken reed that had gone into his hand, or into his heart, rather. Nothing but blank, hopeless ruin stared him in the face. That inward eye saw life spoiled, friends alienated, himself a wretched wanderer, fleeing from his own shadow.

Two hours went by unheeded. Then there came a tap at the door. 'Come in,' he said, mechanically.

'It's locked, sir,' the servant's voice answered. At the same time, Jack was heard scratching and whining outside. Unwillingly Mitchell rose, for the dog's sake. The servant stood outside, holding a tray with a cup and saucer on it.

'Mrs. Clarke asked me to bring this up for you, sir.'

'Well—put it on the table.' He breathed deep, adding: 'Tell her she needn't trouble about anything else to-night.'

'She've gone to bed, sir,' said the girl, her face betraying the nervousness that had allowed her piece of Rothwell grammar to escape.

Genuine Rothwell was the accent, too. Mitchell shrank from it, but exclaimed: 'Gone to bed?'

'She told me I wasn't to say nothing to you, sir, but to bring you this cawfee.'

'She's very good. Tell her not to worry about me.'

The dog came for a talk, when the door was again shut and Mitchell in his chair.

Holding the two paws, and looking sadly into the two eyes, the man soliloquised: '*So you love me still, Jack?* . . . I've lost pretty nearly everything else, old man. And I deserve it. . . . I'm a bully, little dog; a cowardly bully. And poor old Mrs. Clarke has felt it; and yet she doesn't hate me. She's only sorry. . . .' He leaned back wearily, but the dog jumped on to his knees. 'Ah, Jack! if you knew what a low-down brute I am . . . no, not brute. A brute can look you in the face and not feel ashamed. . . . Let's see your eyes, Jack! . . . Ach! love in them. . . . And if 't had been in my way, I suppose I'd have killed that love—poisoned it! . . . Get down, old chap; I'm not good enough!'

He stood up, and tramped about the room, trying to think instead of feel. But no sooner had he sat down again, than the dog returned to him, and more whimsically he recommenced: 'Ah, my little, little god . . . I mean my little dog,' correcting himself with a dreary smile, and breaking off. 'You see, Jack, you've got a god, as you think—he's a mean, contemptible devil, Jack;—but I . . . I've got no guidance at all. . . . And so I come whining to you! . . .'

The summer dusk kept deepening in the room. 'Suppose he'd died,' Mitchell was thinking with horror, when suddenly a yellow gleam from the street lamp, just lit outside, shot up towards the ceiling. He sprang up. 'He may be dying now. . . . I must go and see!' And so hurried from the house.

He dreaded the opening of Thomson's door; but to his hurried question, the maid replied that her master was better.

'Thank God!' There was some mercy left, after all. But now, even as he hastened up the stairs, a new dread seized Mitchell. Had the girl told of that scene in the surgery?

Apparently not. But oh! why had it not been Edith Sanderson there, instead of the woman whose name he was not fit to breathe? And how confidingly, how gladly she smiled to him, with dark eyes and richly burning cheeks! His own burned, at seeing her; but with shame, not gladness.

Somehow Mitchell managed to approach the bed. And there, Thomson, awake and sane, tried to smile at him;—yes, at *him*! 'You're better,' Mitchell murmured, his voice sounding strange to him. He felt the pulse, and then quickly withdrew his hand, saying brokenly some encouraging words.

Mrs. Thomson's face flushed. Grateful tears brightened her eyes, until she hid them, leaning over to kiss her husband. And then,—she had read her husband's thought, perhaps—Mitchell saw her hand steal back, seeking his own. He yielded it, its bony wickedness foully touching the clear softness; it was pressed, and then laid in Thomson's, whose fingers twitched helplessly over it.

Coming away, the doctor knew that his professional habit—there was some value in habit, then, after all?—had preserved him from making a fatal scene of remorse there; but how he had escaped he didn't know. Mrs. Thomson had touched *him*! . . .

On the way home, a wretched woman in the street clutched at him. 'Don't touch me . . . . I don't deserve it!' he groaned between his teeth, hurrying on.

There was a light in Mrs. Clarke's room at the top of the house. Letting himself in, he slowly went up and knocked at her door. If people were to touch him, smile at him, he must somehow make a beginning of crawling up to their level—on his knees, as it were.

XXVI

MITCHELL felt a pang of remorse that his roof should cover a room so bare, so nearly poverty-stricken, as this of his housekeeper's. And yet, he knew that its simplicity was to her taste; for life, to her, consisted not in the number of her possessions. Just such another room, only that morning, had caused him cynical wonder as to what life did consist in under such circumstances. To-night he was readier to learn; and when he left, it was with another kind of wonder, as to the fatuity of his own existence.

The servant, holding a candle, stood by the bed. At sight of her master, she gaped, open-mouthed. Mrs. Clarke's eyes brightened. Clutching the bed-covering round her neck, she half sat up, to show dutiful respect.

'Lie still, lie still!' Mitchell said, deprecatingly.

'O sir—if I'd known you would come! . . . I was just telling Mary about your supper.'

'You take too much trouble about me,' he said gravely. 'Anything will do, Mary.'

Reading his looks, the girl put down the candle, and left. Mitchell drew up a chair to the bedside and sat down, noting with relief that the candle behind him would leave his face dark. It shone full on the housekeeper's. Never before had he seen how old and worn she looked; and although he knew her hair to be grey and scanty, it shocked him to see her so nearly bald. What delight in life could possibly remain for the brain hidden under that hand's-breadth of corpse-coloured skin?

'What's the matter, Mrs. Clarke?' he asked, with an attempt at cheerfulness.

'Never mind me, sir. Do you feel better yourself, now?'

With forced cheerfulness he said: 'The patient doesn't ask the doctor such questions, Mrs. Clarke.' But his heart sank, for he knew that he was on the verge of playing the coward again, and laughing off his recent unkindness to her.

'It grieved me to see you looking so ill this evening,' she persisted.

'And is that what upset you?'

He saw that she would have given much to be able to deny it. He looked down, and said, mumbling: 'I knew it. . . . Only I was . . . I've come to beg your pardon, Mrs. Clarke. I'm ashamed of myself.'

The old woman turned her face from him, and began to sob. Waiting until she should have regained some composure, Mitchell took her hand in his. It was very thin: the veins stood out on it, and the knuckles were protruding and knotted. Yet, as it squeezed his own, his newly quickened faculty was thrilled by the warm, living kindness passing to him through it, as easily as through softer fingers.

Presently she turned her face again, with a look of grateful respect and admiration on it more than he could endure. She held his hand, and he hadn't the heart to remove it; but he felt his ears burn, while he said again, brokenly: 'I'm ashamed of myself, Mrs. Clarke.'

At that, 'I'm sure you no call to be, sir,' she faltered. But there was a touch of apprehensive question in her tone.

He shook his head, answering despondently: 'You don't know, Mrs. Clarke. You don't know.'

'It's not for me to blame you, sir; or try to know, so far as that goes. You always been as kind to me . . .'

She left her sentence incomplete. And for a time there was silence. For the doctor was realising yet another contemplated treachery of his own, in the half-formed scheme of getting the old woman off his hands, with a pension, as if money could have satisfied her faithful soul. In a different spirit, he approached the scheme again; and presently asked: 'How would you and Peter like a comfortable cottage and—say—a couple of pounds a week—at Rothwell?'

He had spoken very kindly, but she looked frightened.

'What, leave you, sir?' she exclaimed.

Considerably damped in spirit, he yet rejoined: 'I'm rather thinking of going away—travelling, you know.'

She fixed her eyes on the opposite wall, and, clutching his hand tighter, seemed to struggle for breath before answering: 'Don't trouble about me, sir. But . . .'—with a piteous glance at him—'but . . . don't do it, sir. Think of yourself. For your own sake.'

'But why not?' he said, puzzled yet uneasy.

'Let an old woman warn you, Doctor Mitchell. It'd break my heart if . . . if . . .' She almost broke down, while Mitchell stared. She gripped his hand again. 'I'd sooner you turned me out, than see you make yourself unhappy that way.'

'What way?' he blurted out; and then, realising at once what he had asked for, shrank from the answer as a criminal shrinks from the damning evidence of his guilt.

But her head shook violently. She turned her face to the wall and moaned: 'I'm a wicked woman to think it, sir; but seeing that photo, and . . . and the rest . . . I couldn't help thinking . . .'

She paused; but Mitchell, more and more humiliated, yet hanging on her words, fascinated to learn how much she had suspected, said: 'Go on . . . I deserve it; and you can't think worse than . . .'

She started up convulsively, letting go his hand, and then, sinking back as though he had struck her: 'Tell me, sir; you haven't—you haven't . . .' Again she paused.

'I haven't *done* anything,' he murmured.

'Thank God!' the old woman sighed. And then it slipped out: 'I was afraid you'd made a wicked woman of her. . . .'

'Good God! . . . No!' he cried, standing up. In a moment, however, he had sat down again, saying abjectly: 'Thank heaven, I've not *done* it. . . . I suppose I meant to . . . Yes; I meant to. O my God!'

The aged, pleading face was turned to him. 'You won't do it, then, sir? You won't go away?'

He sighed. 'Ah, you didn't understand. I was going—to escape. To be out of the way.'

'Then, go, sir! Don't mind me. Go, if she's . . .'

'She? . . . *She* doesn't know! . . . And I'm ashamed for her to see me. . . . I'm not fit to tie up her shoe.'

As he spoke, the threadbare metaphor took fire within him. In fancy he saw her shoe, her foot, and the rich delicate life in her, and loathed himself for having dreamed of sullying it even in a passing thought.

Then he leaned forward, and took the old woman's hand beseechingly. 'You mustn't think anything bad of her.'

She shook her head. 'I was only afraid. . . . You see, sir, she've got no religion . . . if you don't mind my sayin' it, sir?' Her eyes turned on him entreatingly.

'No, my old friend. . . . But she's got . . . something . . . I don't know what it is.' He mused, feeling somehow that it was related to the shame gnawing within himself. 'Like the good, simple-hearted, clean folk at home have got. . . . And I haven't.' He sighed despairingly.

'I think you have, sir,' Mrs. Clarke murmured fondly.

But he rejoined: 'No, *I* haven't. Everybody else, but not me. No, not I,' his thoughts travelled on. 'But the patients I've been despising, and wondering what good they were. *That's* the good. They have it. And they may smile and be kind; and shake hands. . . . And I've lost the right to have people smile at me; oh! and I wanted to make Mrs. Thomson lose it too. . . . I'd better have poisoned her husband's body, than the good in her. . . .'

He roused himself, and met Mrs. Clarke's burning

eyes. 'Would you like what I proposed?' he said.

'Not for me, sir . . .' she began brokenly.

'No; I'm selfish. I was thinking of myself.'

She was silent, looking away from him, for some minutes. At last she said, 'I think—by and by you'd be sorry you'd run away.'

For a moment, while he wondered at her, he said nothing: then, 'Very well. I'll only have a holiday, then. . . . Good-night.'

As he left her, he thought: 'What a blessing to have somebody, strong and sensible, to tell you what to do.'

XXVII

MEANWHILE, a very different scene was enacting at Thomson's house. For, while the doctor upstairs was wishing that he could disappear through the floor down at least as low as the kitchen, there in that kitchen the frightened housemaid was shocking Edith Sanderson by her account of his behaviour in the surgery.

He had departed before Edith, having heard it all, came to tell Hartmann, who, however, was already gone upstairs, to relieve Mrs. Thomson for the night. So Edith waited for her aunt to come down and have some supper.

She waited an hour or more. Then Mrs. Thomson arrived, and exclaimed at finding her still up. 'He seems much better,' she said. 'But I couldn't leave him, until he seemed asleep and settled for the night. You shouldn't have waited. The doctor seems very hopeful now.' With an air of permitting herself at last some relaxation, she leaned one arm across the table, with the other hand deliberately helping herself to some fruit. 'Poor Doctor Mitchell seems very much out of sorts,' she said meditatively.

Edith stood opposite her. She would not even pretend that she had nothing of importance to say, nor yet feel her way diplomatically, as a man would have done. Only, as she stood there, she fidgeted nervously with a fork, afraid to begin.

Soon her aunt noticed, and, looking up, said: 'What is it, Edith?'

'I want to talk to you. I feel I ought to tell you something. I want you to have other advice for uncle.' She blushed furiously. Mrs. Thomson, looking up astonished, saw her white teeth shut tight, and then the thin scarlet lips close firmly.

The elder lady leaned back in her chair, gripping the arms of it, for a moment. 'I suppose,' she said, and her voice had an indignant ring in it, 'you've been listening to Mr. Hartmann. I don't know what his quarrel is with Doctor Mitchell; but . . . perhaps you can tell me, Edith?' She pushed away her plate, and with her elbows on the table, rested her chin on the knuckles of her clenched hands, watching for her niece's reply.

But Edith's task was more awkward than she had anticipated. She hesitated, giving her aunt the opportunity to begin again, more persuasively. 'Mr. Hartmann has been very kind to us,—not more than Doctor Mitchell wanted to be, if I would have let him. Still; he's kind. That doesn't excuse him, though.' Again she leaned back, still watching

Edith's discomfort, and continued: 'I suppose he's jealous, isn't he?'

'Jealous?' The girl turned pale, then reddened again.

'Yes; jealous. And you're encouraging him. . . . But you're trying Doctor Mitchell too much, Edith. I can't think why. He looked wretched to-night. He's worth twenty Hartmanns. In fact, I think it very contemptible of Mr. Hartmann to be working in this underhand way. A man may be jealous—but he shouldn't forget to be a gentleman.' She rose from her scarce-tasted meal, and began methodically to prepare for removing it.

Edith made no attempt to help. She had turned very white, and a dogged expression was hardening in her pale blue eyes. In a moment she laughed unpleasantly. 'I don't know why he should be jealous. *I've* not encouraged Doctor Mitchell. And Ernest knows that. I've promised to marry Mr. Hartmann.' The blood rushed back to her cheeks, but she stood with kindling eyes facing her aunt.

Mrs. Thomson stood with a plate in her hands. 'You've . . . promised . . .' she began slowly; and then, quickening with sudden anger—'And so you two have been flirting by your uncle's sick-bed!'

Edith walked disdainfully to the mantelpiece. Then, over her shoulder, she said coldly: 'You know very well I wouldn't do such a thing. . . . Nor Ernest either! Your favourite Doctor Mitchell might, but Ernest wouldn't and '—she turned, ablaze with anger—'I won't *have* you call him no gentleman!'

Mrs. Thomson began moving the plates again, perhaps under the delusion that she was clearing them away. She said coldly: 'You should have told me, Edith. I didn't know. I had hoped it was going to be Doctor Mitchell. I even thought he seemed like a man in love, never dreaming that you'd throw yourself away.'

Her voice was cruel, and stung the girl to madness. 'He *is* in love!' she said vehemently.

'Poor man! I'm sorry for him.'

'He's in love with *you*!'

'Edith!' Mrs. Thomson set down a handful of forks and spoons as if they were on fire, and turned with burning crimson cheeks to her niece, who, seeing her advantage, went on passionately—

'And I believe he wouldn't care if uncle—I believe he doesn't want uncle to live!'

Mrs. Thomson clenched her two hands tight against her bosom, recoiling from her. 'You—you—you...! How can you dare say such things!'

But her own speech had frightened Edith. Trembling, she leaned her arms on the mantelpiece, and buried her face in them for a moment. Then, 'O aunt, I felt I ought to tell you! . . . I hate to say it; but . . .' And with shamefaced, drooping eyes, hesitating, and clutching the mantelpiece with her fingers, she repeated the story heard from the servant an hour ago. And Mrs. Thomson, her hands on a chair-back, held her breath in listening horror.

But at the end, she sighed, with relief. 'That doesn't prove what you say. It even proves that Doctor Mitchell is terrified at the thought of losing a patient's life. . . . But I suppose you told it to Mr. Hartmann, and he . . .'

The girl replied indignantly, 'I *haven't* told him.

But *last* night, Doctor Mitchell was quite brutal. . . . Oh, I know I'm right.'

Her aunt sat down, fingering at the things on the table. 'I suppose you don't mean wrong. . . . You don't realise what a horrible thing you've said. If I believed it, I'd . . .' Then, with a singular change from vehemence to petulant laugh, 'But I don't believe it, Edith. You haven't convinced me. And I don't think you will.' She smiled thoughtfully at the sole ring on her finger.

Edith felt piqued. 'Hasn't he got a photograph of you?'

Mrs. Thomson looked up, with large, startled eyes. Blushing, she said, 'Yes. I gave it him.' She remembered that she had never seen it in his house, although others were there.

'Do you know,' Edith pursued, for her own justification, 'that he keeps it in a drawer, where he can take it out and . . .'

'And what?' Mrs. Thomson's eyes kindled.

'Oh, *I* don't know,' the girl laughed miserably. 'Kiss it, I suppose.'

'How do you know all this?' Mrs. Thomson stood up, tall and angry.

'I *do* know it,' Edith rejoined, suddenly remembering that she couldn't explain thoroughly without implicating Hartmann. 'The servants are talking about it,' she added viciously.

Mrs. Thomson turned now in earnest to the supper-table. 'You'd better go to bed, Edith. Doctor Mitchell is to be congratulated on escaping you, I think. You're either very wicked, or wickedly foolish. . . . Your uncle's better; and I shall make no change.'

She added, as Edith was going out: 'Stay. If you'll help me clear this away, I'll send your lover down to you. I'm going to be there to-night.'

'You ought to rest, I think.'

'Oh, you've spoilt my rest effectually. Besides of course you want to talk to Mr. Hartmann.'

XXVIII

'EDITH must be mad! There's absolutely no justification at all for what she says,' was Mrs. Thomson's continuous thought when alone by her husband's bedside, after turning out Hartmann, with a low-toned spiteful whisper: 'Your Edith wants you. Leave me here to-night.'

'No justification whatever.' Strong in that conviction, in the dim light, and through the night's stillness that seemed to listen to her thoughts, she reviewed in tumultuous disorder, and with a vividness born of agitation, every incident of her intercourse with Mitchell since they had first met six months ago. Stormy indignation fortified her for several hours; yet gradually she began murmuring, 'I have been to blame, perhaps; but not he.' And later: 'No; he's been a friend. That's all;—a true, dear friend.' Upon that came remembrance of her letter to him. Had it not been too kind? Shrinking from it, yet there seemed no peace possible, until she had remembered every word of it. She sickened upon realising what interpretation might be put upon it, if the friend she had written to were secretly an unscrupulous lover. . . . But Mitchell had made no sign? No; only—she had scarcely seen him since

writing it—until last night! Ah! ... And then?
... Oh, her hand burned as though he were still
holding it! Yet, even then he had taken no smallest
liberty that true friendship would disallow, although
he must have known ...

The summer dawn was awakening. In burning
shame, she was longing wildly for her own room and
thickest darkness, when Hartmann noiselessly came.

'You really *must* go and rest. I'm ashamed ...'
he began.

In a moment she collected herself, and broke in
frigidly: 'Thanks. I can do without your help. ...
You've nothing to be ashamed of, have you? Unless
it is, coming in here.'

'I shall be ashamed if you wear yourself out.'

'Thanks. I wish to be my own mistress here for
the future.'

He shrugged his shoulders. 'Do you want to have
the doctor attending *yourself*?'

It was innocently meant; but she blazed upon
him: 'You're insulting.'

At that, he turned on his heel; yet came back,
pale, and half expecting that she would strike him.
But she had sat down again, for she was trembling.
He took hold of the chair-back, saying, 'I meant no
such thing; and you know it. ... But you must
prove it now, by going.'

A giddiness seized her. She rose, tottering, and
would have fallen, but for his assistance. 'You see,'
he said, 'you're quite done up.' And leading her to
her door, compassion overcame his anger. 'Now
don't worry! I'm not offended. You'll be better
to-morrow.'

Quite unnerved and faint, she fell on her bed, where she shivered so much as to strike terror lest indeed the doctor should have to be called to her. And so she lay, hour after hour, feeling stripped and disgraced. Gradually the sounds of the awakening house came to her. What if her servant should find her there, after having seen Mitchell's extraordinary behaviour of the previous evening? The servants, so Edith said, had been tattling; it would never do for them to see her so distressed at this time!

Hurriedly she undressed, and, getting into bed, lay listening to a neighbouring church bell, ringing for the early Sunday service. The sound carried her thought back to last Sunday—that glorious day at Rothwell, spent in Mitchell's own home, while she could still think of him as her friend. One hour to-day of that splendid peace—what would she not give for it? A longing came over her to sit again listening to the drowsy bees humming in the acacia —a longing the more intense, because she felt that now there could never be the chance to satisfy it. ... Unless she and Fred should go to the Wrights, when he was well? Somehow, she felt as if Fred would be a kind of intruder there. She had not thought of him, so much as . . . ah! so much as of the owner of the house!

And yet, could Mitchell really have been so mad as they said? Searching for grounds of suspicion, she found none—absolutely none. She was working herself into a fever, when suddenly, with the recollection of old Peter's talk, and his actual mention of her own name as the name of Mitchell's hoped-for bride, an explanation of the whole mystery presented itself.

Mrs. Clarke—old busybody Mrs. Clarke—was at the bottom of it all! Yes; it must be so! Had she not once spoken of her fears for her master: of the 'bad woman' who might lead him astray? ... Mrs. Thomson herself was the woman meant! Well, she hid her face in the pillows, with a kind of scornful shame; but could yet afford to laugh, although bitterly, at the relief of finding both herself and her friend exonerated.

Yet, when towards midday Edith came, bringing coffee to her, and saying coldly that the doctor had been and would not need to call again that day, she was aware of an unaccountable satisfaction at the thought that she would be spared the embarrassment of meeting him for a time.

XXIX

BOTH, indeed, were glad when their next visit was over. The lady had flushed and seemed constrained; Mitchell could not imagine why, and it pained him while it satisfied. She, on her side, noticed that he seemed to be acting a part. The more welcome therefore was his announcement that he proposed to start for his holiday on the next day. 'I had a letter Saturday evening, asking if I could push the date forward,' he said; 'and now your husband's out of danger, I shall be glad to go.' He didn't know where he was going.

'To Rothwell?' she suggested, forcing a smile. But he frowned, and looked uncomfortable. 'No. I've written declining that ... I don't know why,' (this with a shrug that deprecated the untruth). He was to be away a month; and, in about three weeks, he had hopes that Thomson might move for a month by the seaside. 'So,' he held out his hand timidly, 'we mayn't meet again for seven or eight weeks.' Her own hand scarcely touched his. They parted, and breathed the more freely at prospect of that long interval to elapse before seeing one another again.

Mitchell being out of the way, and Thomson gaining strength rapidly, the household began gradually to resume its normal condition—at least outwardly. Thomson's pleasure in the engagement between his niece and Hartmann did much towards restoring amicable relations between them and his wife. The old confidence and pleasure in one another's company it could not restore. For one thing, Mrs. Thomson did not share her husband's joy over the engagement. The reason for this, when at last she faced it, caused her many miserable hours. It was simply that she had hoped for Mitchell to be her niece's husband—an innocent hope, surely. Yes; only, her wincing conscience put it to her, whether this preference for Mitchell was quite so harmless as it looked? whether, in fact, there was not in it something more than disinterested admiration of his qualities? Such questions are always unanswerable. She knew it, and she strove to put them away; yet not quite successfully, by reason of a fear she had, that Mitchell might, in his absence, take upon himself to write to her, as a kind of return for her letter from Rothwell. She kept watch on the letter-box; unwilling that the letter, if it came, should fall into Edith's hands; and this stealthy watching had in it an aspect of guilt just enough to reawaken all the troublesome questions she would fain have left to sleep.

However, no letter came. But this, added to anxious inquiries from the Wrights as to what had become of Mitchell, corroborated to a certain extent her own apprehensions that something was very much amiss with the man. He was travelling on the Continent, his substitute said: and that was all she knew. In course of time, although she was quite unconscious of having changed her opinion, she began to think of Mitchell rather pityingly, as the man who had unwarrantably fallen in love with her. She would have preferred to forget him.

That, however, was impossible. Her convalescent husband was often speaking of the gratitude they owed the doctor. It was hard to satisfy him; and Mrs. Thomson constantly feared that Edith would allow her dislike for Mitchell to be too obvious to her uncle. In fact, he noticed it. One afternoon, when his restored health was enabling him fully to enjoy the last week of their stay by the sea, he said, as they were moving from the beach: 'I'm sure of my tea—so I've only one wish just at present.'

They laughed. 'What's that?'

'Why, I feel like a boy again.' He stooped to pick up a stone, and fling it into the retreating water, and his wife smiled: 'I believe you are a boy.'

'Well, at any rate, I should like a game at cricket on this sand, this evening;—there's another wish, so I have two. And if only Mitchell were here—*that's* what I want. I should like to find him waiting for us when we go in.'

Edith exclaimed: 'Should you? I'm sure I don't want to see him!' She flushed angrily; and soon walked on ahead with Hartmann.

'What makes Edith so bitter against Mitchell?' Thomson asked his wife.

She stood still, breathing apprehensively; and, while he stooped to pick up another stone, faltered: 'It's so . . . silly.'

He stood up. 'Well?' he asked, and saw that she had flushed and was avoiding his eyes.

Looking straight away at the horizon, she responded: 'I . . . I can't tell you what it is, Fred. It's something I can't say.' Her glance turned rapidly upon him, and away again. For she had seen in his face no readiness to understand. His eyes had twinkled at her humorously, and his lips were drawn up into an expression of mock solemnity.

They walked on some distance.

At last he said insinuatingly: 'I always thought that Mitchell and you were such chums.'

Her persistent silence incited him to tease her, and he continued laughingly: 'In fact, when you were away, I fancied he missed you as much as I did. I said something of the sort to Edith.'

'*You* said *that*?' she exclaimed.

'Well?' said her husband, astonished to see that her colour rose suddenly, and that she bit her lip.

Nothing more was said then. Their meal was constrained. Mrs. Thomson felt that this secret was pushing her and Fred as far asunder as they had ever been. Yet what could she do?

But after supper, Edith and Hartmann went out for a stroll. Thomson drew his chair to the open window, where he could sit and watch the moonlight on the water. He lit a pipe, and wished that his wife seemed more at ease; for her silence made him fearful of some uncomfortable display of emotion to follow it.

He was not mistaken. Having provided herself with some knitting, she drew a hassock near him, and sat down at his feet. But, instead of proceeding quietly with her work, she put an arm affectionately over his knees; feeling despairingly that no caress could serve instead of confidence between them.

'Well?' he said, at last.

Her only reply was to stroke his knee more affectionately.

'I suppose,'—he spoke almost reproachfully—'you want to tell me what it is between you and Mitchell?'

She dropped her knitting, and turned so that she could look up into his face. 'I wish I could; but I . . . I daren't, Fred!'

The lamp on the table behind him shone full upon her: on her face and throat, as she threw back her head and met his eyes, as though bidding him to look her through and through and find her faultless.

He laid down his pipe, and took both her hands, smiling as if she were a child. 'I can't understand it, Nan. I should have said he was half in love with you. I've more than once thought it would be strange if he weren't.'

Her eyes closed for a moment painfully, but at once were yielded to his scrutiny again. But her panting, and her sudden colour, would have been admissions that his guess was correct, without her words: 'I'm afraid he is, Fred.'

Her beauty struck him. 'I don't wonder,' he said, yet laughing a little cynically. 'Only'—and now he let go her hands, feeling for his pipe—'don't tell me that he's—ah—misbehaved—in any way.'

Scorn flashed momentarily in her face. 'Do you think I'd let him?'

Again he laughed. 'I don't believe he'd try, Nan. He's a good fellow. . . . In fact,' stroking her hair, 'I don't blame him. Why shouldn't he admire you? . . . It isn't as if he . . .' Here he stopped to relight his pipe. A broad smile overspread his features; and, puffing out a cloud of smoke with admiring satisfaction, he went on—'as if he'd been a blackguard. . . . Now, I was in his power six weeks ago. He might have . . .' He laughed excitedly.

'O Fred! Fred!' she cried, burying her face on his knees.

Suddenly, exasperated, he exclaimed: 'But, hang it, Nan! you don't suppose I mean it?'

Her head was violently shaken. 'I don't,' she sobbed. 'No . . . but . . . Edith . . .'

'Edith! Get up. You must tell me now.'

At that she sat up; and, taking his hand, hurriedly told him the outlines of the affair in the surgery, as she had heard it from Edith. But in her agitation several points were forgotten. She had said nothing of the photograph, when Fred stood up, saying impatiently: 'Well, well, you've said quite enough. I'm ashamed of you both. . . . It's just a woman's way. There's not a particle, not the shadow of a reason, that I can see, for distrusting the man. In fact, all you've said tells on his side. And yet you harbour these silly suspicions!'

O

Edith and Hartmann returning, cut short the discussion, and it was never resumed.

And the results of it were unhappy. Mrs. Thomson's conscience was tortured by the thought that she had made but half a confession after all. She had meanly, contemptibly shielded herself and her own indiscretions. That thought by itself was enough to make her uneasy, when alone with her husband. But besides that, she was vexed by his behaviour.

For, however reasonable it might be in him, she yet resented the tolerance he had shown. If he cared for her more, would he not have been angry at the very mention of Mitchell's suspected love? Would he at any rate have professed, so aggressively as he now began to do, his admiration and friendship for the doctor? She at least could not and would not tolerate such things: and this sense of opposition in opinion was intensely painful to her.

A sullen, brooding anger against Mitchell himself grew up in her. At first, she had vaguely pitied him; but that sentiment died away. She left off blaming herself, no longer realising that on her account he might be very miserable.

XXX

AND Mitchell? Dogged by the shadow of the crime he had so nearly committed, and of which he had in fact been guilty in desire, he was for a time incapable of rest, and hurried from place to place seeking only forgetfulness. His own society was unbearable; yet several times, having for a while forgotten himself in the chance companionship afforded by hotels, some small act of kindness suddenly horrified him by its contrast with the smear of disgrace across his consciousness, and he withdrew to the company of his own miserable thoughts, which at least knew the worst of him.

Slowly, however, the horror receded, giving place to the less acute but more continuous pain of melancholy. And here, it was the thought of that undefined excellence in Mrs. Thomson—viewed not by intellect, but by the faculty quickened in him in the surgery that evening—that saved him. He would have drowned care in riotous living; only he felt that that would be sacrificing his right, even to think from afar of what was beginning to appear to him the one worthy thing in the world. In so deciding, it seemed that he was clinging desperately to the sole link by which he was still connected with ordinary wholesome people.

That mere wholesomeness, faithfulness, of social intercourse—he had overlooked it, when wondering of late why his patients should seek to live, or what end their lives served. Light dawned on him, through this melancholy, which confronted him with yet another temptation. Not, indeed, to make away with himself—that were a coward's trick—but, to disappear; to begin a fresh existence, reckless, adventurous, risking his life. . . . He resisted, mindful of his duty to Mrs. Clarke, who was dependent on him. Her affection was now, perhaps, his most precious possession, since he dared not count on his friends at Rothwell, and had lost his right to anything but disgust from the Lane Thomsons.

This idea expanded as time went on. All round

him, wherever men and women were, he saw signs of the same exquisite thing. Rich or poor, healthy or diseased, they cherished still something analogous to Mrs. Clarke's faithful love for himself: connected somehow with his own new-found power of appreciating it. It was an instinct—he could call it nothing else—asserting itself through them: mastering them, domineering over them, just as, thank Heaven! in himself it had in the nick of time arisen and thrown off the control of his superficial desires. . . . As the notion gained in clearness, he began to long for his holiday's end, that he might return and set to work again, saving from death the bodies in which for the time being that instinct dwelt; bodies no longer, in his eyes, wretched machines for producing their own sustenance, but vehicles of laughter, kindly looks, friendly hand-grasps, love.

Still, the feeling was fitful. After restoring his self-esteem, for days it left him; and then he would grow despondent. For, believing once more in himself, he one day detected that self in the act of dramatising something very suspiciously like a love-scene with Mrs. Thomson. He had made himself very tired, and started horrified from a day-dream—or rather, a late-evening dream after wine—in which her head was on his shoulder, and she was saying something more than flattering.

The poison was in his blood, then? It seemed so. Yet, if that desired joy might be his once—only once—he would be—ah! would he be?—content. As it was, it could never happen; and he was doomed to a barren, incomplete existence after all.

But, when the time arrived, he hastened back to

London, eager to see Mrs. Clarke; and jealous that the *locum tenens* should usurp any longer the privilege of doing that work for which alone life seemed worth living in the future.

He had been in London a fortnight before the Lane Thomsons returned; and his work, he thought, had fully restored his sanity. At any rate, he could now disentangle the threads of his recent aberration, and some of them he could view without shame.

Not that he had lost at all his detestation of those treacherous desires regarding Lane Thomson. Recollection of them still prostrated him at times; and sometimes, too, he ground his teeth, realising the folly of having wished to gain Mrs. Thomson's love. But, on the other hand, he was no longer ashamed of having loved her. It was so natural a thing to do. In fact, he loved her still; and rejoiced in doing so, feeling sure of his self-control.

And yet the Thomsons' return agitated him. He would have liked to avoid them, had there been any plausible excuse for such behaviour. But then, he had to consider, what would the Wrights say?—not to speak of acquaintances whose talk, in that case, might be disagreeable to Mrs. Thomson.

XXXI

EVENTS proved that there was some cause for his timidity. Their first evening together was uncomfortable, constrained; but, being quite unaware of any reason for this on his friends' side, Mitchell attributed the discomfort to his own mood. All of them, probably, owed more than they suspected to the force of custom. There are certain conventions of society which seem like an expression of the common will of our race, in their imperious disregard of individual feelings—conventions which, as Thomson might have said, demand a kind of hypocrisy from the individual, unless he is happy enough to find his inmost desires in harmony with this common-sense of mankind. Thomson was skilful enough to make use of these conventions, in much the same fashion as a sailor makes use of the trade-winds, or a farmer the summer. Thanks to his tact, Time was able to do its glacier-like work, slowly smoothing away the obstructions in their intercourse. Even Edith Sanderson had no choice but to be superficially agreeable to the doctor.

But Thomson could not fail to observe a change in his friend—just such a change, he was obliged to think, as would be accounted for by what had been hinted of him. Mitchell was less dogmatic than before; and certainly more kindly. The melancholy that tinged his manner took Thomson's fancy; so that, as before he had never blamed the man, so now he was sincerely sorry for him. Once or twice, remembering how his own behaviour had fallen under Mitchell's censure, he smiled to himself: 'I shouldn't wonder if the fellow really wished me out of the way. How he must have despised me! . . . Does now, very likely!'

It would have pleased him to behave a little more sympathetically to his wife; but pride withheld him. Since that evening, she had never spoken of the doctor; and Thomson shrugged his shoulders, silently blaming her unexpressed resentment. He had thought her more generous.

She also had seen that Mitchell was altered. His eyes, she thought, were curiously like his own little dog's eyes. But the cold anger in her heart was feeding on the estrangement from her husband, which she could not forgive Mitchell for having caused. She was sorry for him for a little while; then she grew impatient, and at length came to despise and distrust him.

For, partly to tease her and Edith, partly to assert himself, and again partly to show his confidence in Mitchell, Thomson took to making in the doctor's presence covert allusions to the matter that was disturbing them; and he was genuinely amused by their ingenuity in escaping from the embarrassment. And his wife, supposing that he mistrusted her and desired to watch her, retired more and more frigidly into herself, secretly criticising Mitchell's poorness of spirit. If he was innocent, she reasoned, why did he not resent her husband's conduct? Or, on the other hand, if guilty, why did he submit himself to it, coming there with his mournful eyes? Why, unless he still harboured his loathsome desire? . . . Oh! and why did her own husband encourage this man? She for her part had lost all confidence in him, and with it all comfort in his society.

Yes; that friendship was dead. And its dead body was lying in the road of her friendship with the Wrights, whose anxious and puzzled inquiries about Mitchell she could not answer. A letter to Emily Wright was a pain to her now. And when she tried to find strength in her notion of Duty— duty to a husband who distrusted her—even that last comfort was marred for her by the recollection that she had really obtained the idea of it from Doctor Mitchell.

If only he had been in reality what at first he seemed! She tried one evening to think of him more generously. It was late in November. His year in London was nearly run out; and she would not see him many more times before the Wrights would have returned, and would be desiring her to think well of him. She would like, she felt, to be able to gratify them, if it were but for the sake of peace at last. She had begun to live on the hope of that—of mere peace. Mitchell once gone, and Edith and Hartmann gone too, she would be alone with her husband for the rest of her life: an unsatisfying existence, no doubt, but at least free from the miserable agitations of the last few months. Merely to do her dreary, lifelong duty would demand so much fortitude, that she took a kind of pride in facing the task. And it would help her, if she were able to think of Mitchell and of her pleasant days at Rothwell, sometimes.

Truly, on this evening she thought him more like himself—possibly because she wished to think so. They were quite merry at supper. Hartmann was away arranging about a house in preparation for his marriage; and Thomson, beaming with fun, was slily teasing Edith with suggestions that her lover had given her the slip. Her laughter, her blushes, and her glistening eyes, wrought upon him to produce variations of their charm. Momentary reserve, sudden coolness, a flash of scorn breaking again into smiles and deeper blushes—very brilliant under the lamp-light—were obtained; and after supper Thomson endeavoured to draw Mitchell into complicity with him.

'Be prepared, my poor girl. You should always have a willow-wreath or two in readiness, in London. You can't trust these city men, you know. Mitchell will tell you that. Character deteriorates in the town: if you want honest faithfulness, you must look for it in the country.'

Thomson seemed unconscious that his speech might give pain; but his wife avoided looking at Mitchell, who frowned, muttering rather bitterly, 'I'm afraid that's truer than you think.'

To the lady it sounded like an admission of his own backsliding—a sign of grace, perhaps.

But Edith, with a touch of disdain, said: 'Try to be polite, Doctor Mitchell. We're talking of Mr. Hartmann.'

Her uncle turned to her, explaining: 'Mitchell's not been long enough in London, Edith, to have thoroughly deteriorated into politeness. I fear he's a hopeless case, too: you can see that he's been pining for weeks to get back to his unsophisticated country-folk.'

This was a new idea to Mrs. Thomson. A feeling rushed over her that she had been unjust. What right had she ever had to suspect this man's friendship? He was suffering an exile's unhappiness; and she had wilfully misconstrued it into guilt. She glanced at her husband and said: 'If you knew those people at Rothwell, Fred, and how fond they are of the doctor, you wouldn't wonder that he wants to leave us and get back to them.' As she finished, her eyes turned to Mitchell, and there was friendship swimming in them. Her face, too, was brilliant with it.

And Mitchell, gladdening, replied awkwardly: 'Oh,—I didn't say anything about being glad to leave here.'

Thomson turned again to Edith. 'After all,' he said solemnly, 'Mitchell has degenerated. The true rustic would say plainly, "I don't care tuppence about leaving you. . . ." But our friend here prevaricates.' He smiled round upon Mitchell; 'Still, I suppose you'll soon pick up the old straightforwardness, doctor? You've only to go round, and when you see a spade, say, "That's a spade," and so on.'

Edith Sanderson tossed her pretty head. 'It's delightfully simple, I should think, uncle.'

Mrs. Thomson looked up from her work to smile to Mitchell, and say, 'Can you forgive their ignorance? They haven't been to Rothwell.'

'Well for our manners that we've not,' rejoined the husband. 'Ignorance, indeed! But they don't appreciate us, Edith. Let's leave them alone. I want some music; and it may soothe your forsaken soul too, my poor girl. Come along!'

'Bother!' exclaimed Mrs. Thomson. 'Why can't you be contented here?' She looked up at him with a provoking smile.

'"Bother"? My dear wife! What, "bother" music? Now, if 't had been Mitchell . . .' He was standing on the hearthrug, swaying rhythmically backwards and forwards: and now he looked down at the doctor. 'By the way—it's a singular thing, your noted impatience of music, Mitchell. And—yes, I'm coming, Edith.' He went to her, and put her arm within his, saying: 'Don't worry about that rascal Hartmann, my love,' then turned to admonish Mitchell, continuing: 'Your dislike for music, Mitchell, makes me suspicious of your bucolic simplicity. In fact, treasons, stratagems, and spoils . . .'

Mrs. Thomson, catching Mitchell's uneasy glance, rose, dropping a cotton reel, as she said impatiently: 'You talk too much, Fred.'

Mitchell stooped to pick up the cotton reel which had rolled under his chair. But he heard Thomson saying, 'Well, well. No, don't disturb yourselves. I know you two would sooner be alone, to talk about the country.' And when he arose, Thomson and Edith were going down the stairs, and the lady was standing waiting for him with angry cheeks. The husband's voice reached them. 'I'm a poor, neglected husband, Edith. . . .'

Mitchell frowned. 'Let me carry something for you,' he said, laying hands on the work-basket.

'Thanks. I'd rather take it myself.'

At that moment Thomson returned. 'He's come to watch me,' his wife thought. But he said merrily, 'Now—*don't* disturb your *tête-à-tête*. I only want a cigarette.'

But as he went to the mantelpiece, Mitchell shut the door. 'Look here, Thomson. I want a word with you alone.'

Thomson turned round astonished, his face shining fierce red; but his wife, throwing down her work with a frightened cry, sprang to him and seized his arm. 'No, Fred! No! Don't listen to him. Don't believe him. I know all about him. I've told you!' She turned to face Mitchell. She understood his behaviour now! He had been trying insidiously to alienate her and Fred.

'You've . . . told . . . ?' Mitchell began; and Thomson's face darkened as he looked at his wife.

But she, almost choking with anger: 'I know what you were going to say, Doctor Mitchell, and I forbid you to say it! We know what you are!'

Mitchell had never felt so thoroughly frightened; but he found force to say, 'I don't know what you think me . . . I could defend . . . But it isn't worth while. I'll go.'

Thomson took a step forward. He stammered pitifully, saying: 'No, my friend! you—you—I must have an explanation now.' He turned to his wife, who had not taken her eyes from the discomfited doctor. 'And you, Nan—what is it you don't wish him to say to me? What is there you haven't told me? Is there . . . ?'

She was looking straight and scornfully into his eyes as she began: 'There is noth—.' Then her face turned crimson. She bit her lip, and, looking down, began to tap her foot nervously on the carpet. For she had remembered that Fred had never been told of Mitchell's possession of her photograph. Several moments she stood drooping; then, still looking down, she faltered: 'He may tell you what he likes. But if he says I don't love you—O Fred! Fred!—it isn't true.'

With one piteous glance at her husband she moved towards the door, which Mitchell held open for her. She gave him no look, shrinking aside as she passed him, and holding her dress away for fear it should touch him.

At the same moment, the two men heard Hartmann come in from the street and enter the room where Edith was at the piano. Her music ceased as Mitchell shut the door and locked it.

'I suppose we may as well sit down,' said Thomson in his coolest, thinnest tone. And he curled himself into a big easy-chair by the fire, throwing his legs over one of its arms.

Mitchell sat down, keeping his back straight and his shoulders square, and muttering, 'You may be showing me the door in five minutes.'

The other carefully adjusted the tips of his fingers together, and, looking at them, rejoined: 'Oh—if you have done her any wrong, my friend, I shall deliberately hunt you down and ruin you;—unless . . .' Suddenly he rolled round in the chair, straightened his legs on the hearthrug, shoved his hands deep into his trouser pockets, and cried: 'Unless—O my God! —unless she loves you! I'd spare you then.' His eyes blazed steadily on Mitchell, eager for his answer.

Mitchell looked at him, but felt a twitching of his lips as he said slowly: 'Aren't you satisfied with what you heard her say just now? She's eating her heart out for a little show of love from you.'

Thomson's eyes gleamed gratification. To conceal it, he leaned forward and began stirring the fire. Mitchell noticed that his hand shook violently, and waited, in vain trying to keep his own knees from trembling.

At last the other stood up, and, turning, said in a high-pitched, peevish tone: 'I hope you're going to put matters straight, my friend'; adding, with a weak attempt at a smile, 'Is it something very dreadful?'

Mitchell frowned, and, looking into the fire, muttered: 'I was simply going to tell you that you're a fool.'

Thomson laughed hysterically.

'But my wife—she's implicated somehow, you see. What is it she hasn't told me?'

Mitchell leaned back, and, looking up at Thomson, asked bitterly: 'What is it she *has* told you?'

The other, trying to speak, shook his head. He had to sit down before his voice would come, and then it was thin, deprecatory, and broken. 'You've brought it on yourself, Mitchell. . . . I . . . I . . . understand that you're . . .' With a braggart laugh, his voice suddenly deepened. 'Oh! hang it, man! I'm ashamed to repeat such woman's folly;—she had an idea you were in love with her.'

Affecting to laugh, he attempted to pour himself out some whisky. But he spilt some and desisted, when Mitchell, standing up, mumbled: 'I have been. But I can't think how she . . .'

'You've given her no reason?' interrupted Thomson quickly.

'Not the slightest,' said the doctor, with a relieved sigh.

Thomson laughed. 'Well then, what harm's done? . . . Here, have some whisky? And you're not smoking!' He began to chuckle gleefully, and then, with the accent of impatience, continued: 'My wife has got more sense than any woman I know. Still, she remains a woman. Her conscience, for instance, is most inconvenient. There's some little thing worrying her that she wishes to tell me;—you noticed?'

Mitchell shrugged his shoulders. 'I haven't the faintest idea . . .' he began uneasily.

'My dear fellow, of course you haven't. No mere man can understand the feminine conscience. Why, when she told me of this—it was when we were away—she felt herself impelled to tell me another thing—quite irrelevant—about a little accident you had in mixing some medicine for me.'

Mitchell started up. 'Good God! ... Did she hear of that? It wasn't quite irrelevant.'

Thomson turned pale, then flushed. 'Well, but—man alive! what do you mean? Didn't you save my life?'

'I did all that was possible for you,' Mitchell groaned; 'but . . .' He turned, and hid his face in his arms on the table.

Thomson clutched his arm, and shook him. 'But—but—you—you—you mean to say—the other thought occurred to you?'

Without showing his face, Mitchell nodded; and so remained for some minutes. Then he said: 'It came into my mind when I was putting that stuff ready for you.'

When he looked up, Thomson, pale and trembling, was watching him, and said, breathing hard: 'I've already thought that perhaps it went somehow like that. . . . But I hadn't realised it before;—no, not quite realised it. . . . Give me time. . . .' He stood up, and began walking backwards and forwards. Then, his voice squeaking in excitement: 'Look here, Mitchell. I've always believed in you and liked you—though you've been damned unpleasant at times! But—I owe my life to you, man! You hated that idea, didn't you? Oh—I've seen it. You've been in hell for it. . . . Well, then, don't you see, any man in your place might have been visited by such a thought; but you didn't act upon it! That's the point!'

Mitchell sat up, looking at the fire miserably. He was deadly pale. Then he rose, and said, 'I suppose I'd better go.'

'Go? Not at all! . . . You've nothing to be ashamed of, have you? You don't wish it *now* . . . ?'

'O God! not now.' He sat down again irresolutely; and Thomson came and sat opposite, looking into his eyes, and at last Mitchell turned to meet his look, saying: 'You're a better man than me, Thomson. I was going to find fault with you about your behaviour, but . . . the way you've taken this . . .'

Thomson laughed uncomfortably. 'Oh, I've had time to think it over. That's part of my reprehensible behaviour! It's better than emotion.'

Mitchell shook his head. 'And yet—it was emotion that saved me.'

'I should have thought 'twas reason.'

'No; emotion. And a kind of feeling, too, that your—that Mrs. Thomson . . . that 'twas better to . . .'

Thomson, waiting for his conclusion, at last said: 'Help yourself to some whisky'; and going to the door, he opened it and called—'Nan!'

Mitchell stood up. 'You'd better let me clear out,' he said.

But almost immediately Mrs. Thomson stood at the door—pale-faced, and with lifted head. Her eyes shone inquiry—to her husband.

He began: 'Well, Nan, it's all right. What you told me was true enough, in a way . . .'

'Then why hasn't Doctor Mitchell gone?' she said acidly.

Her husband paused a moment, and then said, a

little angrily: 'I'll endeavour to explain, if you will be reasonable.'

Her face grew hot, and anger flashed in her eyes. 'Thanks; I'm tired of reason. There's no room for it here. He's tried to come between me and you. . . . I don't know—I'm ashamed to think—what he must have taken me for—and I loathe it! I loathe it! I want never to see him again!'

'My dear wife!' Thomson began, 'you're outrageous!' Then, coldly, he went on: 'It's your own unreasonableness that's to blame now—not Mitchell. If you care to please me . . .'

'I can't live in the way you mean, Fred!' she cried imploringly, throwing her wrists over his shoulders. 'I can't! I can't! It's all false and hollow, without the other.'

Thomson shrugged his shoulders, looking ruefully at the doctor.

The latter had clenched his teeth. Now he laughed bitterly. 'Your wife's quite right, Thomson. I deserve it. . . . But you've been a man to me to-night.' He held out his hand.

'I can't—I really can't let you go like this!'

'You can't stop me.' And, in the midst of Thomson's protestations, he left.

As he passed out of the house, the sound of Edith's piano-playing reached his ears, although not his consciousness. It was not until he had walked himself weary, and, coming home, had burnt Mrs. Thomson's photograph and her letters, that the music recurred to him. It lulled him to sleep; and in the morning he awakened with it, conscious of its quiet, pastoral feeling—a feeling of late summer evening, and of peaceful life in old farm-houses. Contrasting with his own recently fevered existence, it put that in a new unholy light. Could anything beautiful, he wondered, come of such a life as he had been living? For answer, there was the misery he had left, had intensified, between the Lane Thomsons.

But out of the simple, old-fashioned English life suggested by the music (he imagined his own village, centuries ago), how much that was strenuous and beautiful had come! And if, notwithstanding the frippery of modern fashion, Mrs. Thomson's prejudices were of the old-fashioned sort, was it not better for her so?

But he sighed, thinking of her unhappiness with it all.

XXXII

No efforts that Thomson made could induce his wife to see Mitchell again; although, in the reaction from that evening's anger, her resentment towards the doctor disappeared. 'I can't forgive myself, Fred,' she confessed. 'I've let him spoil his life—and I've lost him as a friend. But—I can't quite forgive him, either. You must give way to my weakness on this point. As it is, I can respect him; but I know if I met him . . . I should feel disgraced, Fred. You may tell him that, if you like.' Her husband yielded, but shook his head. 'I confess I don't understand you in the least degree,' he said.

When Hartmann arranged to get away a few days before Christmas, and introduce Edith to his family in Yorkshire, Mrs. Thomson secretly rejoiced. They would not return until the new year; and she counted much on having the house to herself when the Wrights came. For Wright, eager for time with Mitchell, had engaged a substitute to do the Rothwell work, and was coming to London on the day when Hartmann left. Under the circumstances, nothing could be better, Mrs. Thomson thought. Emily Wright's sympathy was becoming all but necessary to her, in the absence of sympathetic understanding from any other quarter.

To Mitchell, the prospect of meeting his friends was less pleasing. They arrived late in the afternoon, two days before Christmas Day; and in one way or another—by dint of play-acting—he contrived to be cheerful during their prolonged tea-time. There was, fortunately, the baby to be admired and made much of. He did it; not easily, knowing that all the while Wright was narrowly observing him.

It was suggested that they should go and have supper at the Lane Thomsons'. Mitchell said: 'Yes; go by all means. I shan't be able.' He had in fact carefully provided a professional excuse, that served to satisfy Mrs. Wright, although she was disappointed. Her husband was not so easily hoodwinked. He guessed that Mitchell wanted time alone with him; and the two started for an hour's walk. Emily Wright, after putting the baby to bed, was to go on at once to the other house, where her husband would join her later.

The two men had reached Charing Cross Bridge —they chose that direction by a common impulse— before Mitchell could come to the point. There, watching the black river and the lights on the other bridge, as they had done a year ago, he told his story.

When he had ended, Wright only sighed. They strolled along again three or four minutes, before he spoke; and then it was only to say softly: 'Old man, I used to *think* I loved you. But I never did, until now.'

Another silence followed. Then Mitchell said: 'I should like to get away to-morrow.'

'We'll see. . . . I may tell Emily about it?'

Mitchell hesitated. 'I suppose you'd better. Yes. Don't go having secrets from her. I've made one good woman miserable, as it is.'

'Emily will put that all right,' said the other.

'Perhaps. Mrs. Thomson'll never be happy, though. Thomson's a good fellow—but . . .'

'I know,' Wright assented. 'I'm sorry for her.'

'And yet—I don't know that it matters. She's more reason to be satisfied than most of us.'

'Hm! . . . I don't see it.'

'Do you remember our talk on the bridge—a year ago? I wanted something inclusive. . . . I'm nearer to it, thanks to this business. And she's never been far away from it.'

'Well?'

'No—I can't tell you the philosophy of it now. Some other time, perhaps . . . But, look here: Mrs. Thomson's horror of me—and her sense of duty—are not whims; not prejudices. . . .'

'I don't see how you know that.'

'Well, if they are—don't you see that a prejudice can't grow out of nothing? Its roots must be alive, at any rate. I seem to see that these things are—

intrinsic, in her: they're necessary, inevitable. Not so much views held by her; but—like the sap that runs up a tree into one of the leaves. I fancy she's nearer the centre of things than most of us.'

. . . . .

About the time that Mitchell reached his home on the following evening, Mrs. Thomson, alone with her regained friend, was saying: 'Will you let him know that I'm sorry? And that I believe in him now? I'm so glad Mrs. Clarke told you.'

'You will see him yourself, sometime.'

'No—I'd rather not see him. I'm settling down, Emily, into the old life.'

'The old life, dear?'

'Why not?'

'I hoped you were . . .'

'No, dear. I see it now. Fred and I are not made alike. We shall never quite agree.' She shuddered, and pressed her fingers over her eyes. 'We misunderstood Doctor Mitchell; but, seeing what we took him to be, Fred ought not to have liked him.'

'Oh, but—Annie!'

'But—would you like me, Emily—if *I* hadn't cared? If I tolerated what—what I thought of him —and, and—played the piano and drawled about art and fashion, and was all wrong in myself?'

Mrs. Wright leaned forward, looking into the fire. Then she said: 'But there's no harm in these things.'

'I know. They're good, in their way: but not necessary, like the other. If we're right — I can't tell you what that means, but I know and you know —then it doesn't matter what else we are. . . . I'm beginning to envy old Mrs. Clarke—although she's got nothing that we generally think necessary. . . . Did you say her old brother was dying?'

'I doubt if she will find him alive to-night.'

There was a long pause. Then Mrs. Thomson mused: 'Poor old man! I don't forget what he said to me. . . . I think there's something else lives, Emily, besides *people*. His simplicity and faithfulness, for instance. Dear old Mrs. Clarke has it, too: and you see, you tell me, she's passed it on to Doctor Mitchell: and the love for it has come to me. . . .'

Mrs. Wright took her hand. 'And are you going to live on that, Annie?'

There was a smile, and a sob. 'I'm going to try.'

Printed by T. and A. CONSTABLE, Printers to Her Majesty
at the Edinburgh University Press

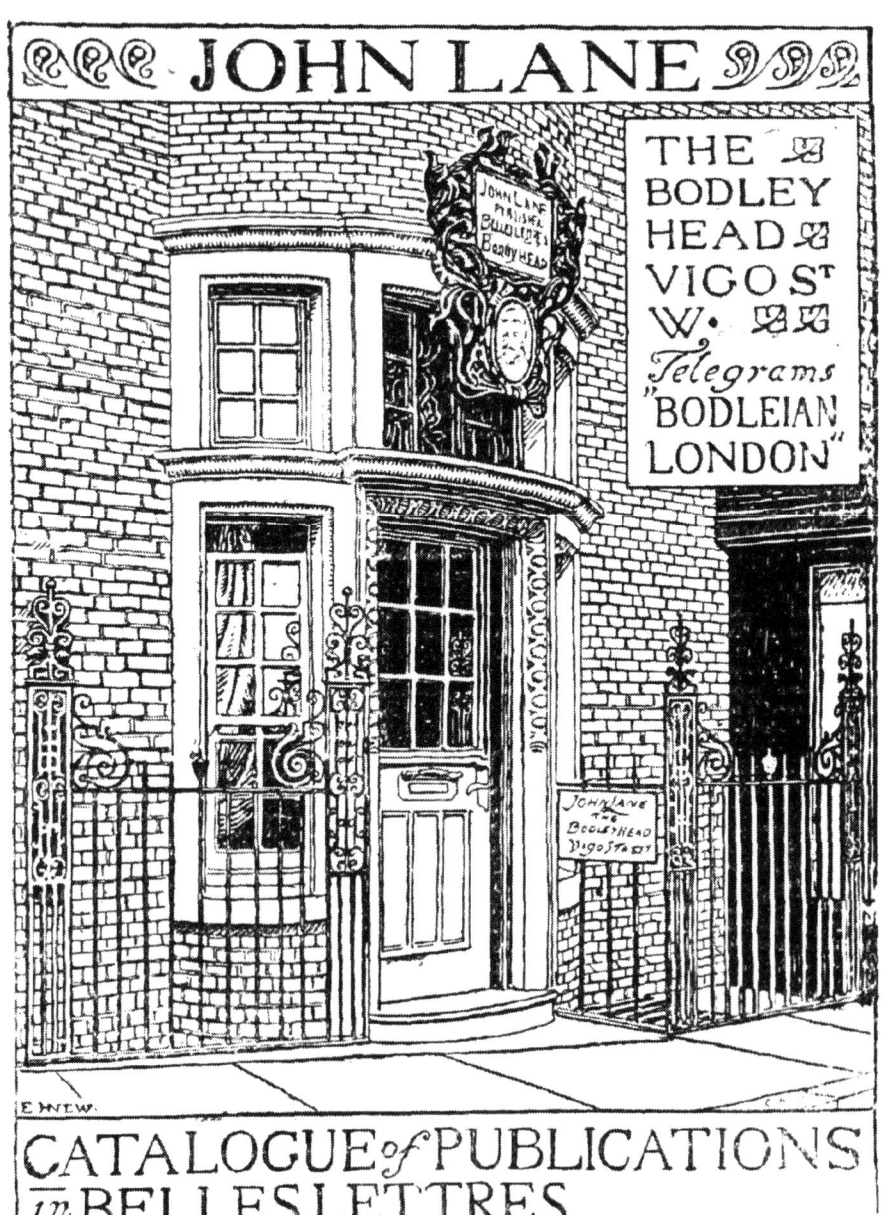

List of Books
IN
BELLES LETTRES
Published by John Lane
𝔗𝔥𝔢 𝔅𝔬𝔡𝔩𝔢𝔶 𝔥𝔢𝔞𝔡
VIGO STREET, LONDON, W.

Adams (Francis).
ESSAYS IN MODERNITY. Crown 8vo. 5s. net. [*Shortly.*
A CHILD OF THE AGE. Crown 8vo. 3s. 6d. net.

A. E.
HOMEWARD: SONGS BY THE WAY. Sq. 16mo, wrappers, 1s. 6d. net. [*Second Edition.*
THE EARTH BREATH, AND OTHER POEMS. Sq. 16mo. 3s. 6d. net.

Aldrich (T. B.).
LATER LYRICS. Sm. fcap. 8vo. 2s. 6d. net.

Allen (Grant).
THE LOWER SLOPES: A Volume of Verse. Crown 8vo. 5s. net.
THE WOMAN WHO DID. Crown 8vo. 3s. 6d. net. [*Twenty-third Edition.*
THE BRITISH BARBARIANS. Crown 8vo. 3s. 6d. net. [*Second Edition.*

Atherton (Gertrude).
PATIENCE SPARHAWK AND HER TIMES. Crown 8vo. 6s. [*Third Edition.*

Bailey (John C.).
ENGLISH ELEGIES. Crown 8vo. 5s. net. [*In preparation.*

Balfour (Marie Clothilde).
MARIS STELLA. Crown 8vo. 3s. 6d. net.

Beeching (Rev. H. C.).
IN A GARDEN: Poems. Crown 8vo. 5s. net.
ST. AUGUSTINE AT OSTIA. Crown 8vo, wrappers. 1s. net.

Beerbohm (Max).
THE WORKS OF MAX BEERBOHM. With a Bibliography by JOHN LANE. Sq. 16mo. 4s. 6d. net.
THE HAPPY HYPOCRITE. Sq. 16mo. 1s. net.

Bennett (E. A.).
A MAN FROM THE NORTH. Crown 8vo. 3s. 6d. [*In preparation.*

Benson (Arthur Christopher).
LYRICS. Fcap. 8vo, buckram. 5s. net.
LORD VYET AND OTHER POEMS. Fcap. 8vo. 3s. 6d. net.

Bridges (Robert).
SUPPRESSED CHAPTERS AND OTHER BOOKISHNESS. Crown 8vo. 3s. 6d. net. [*Second Edition.*

Brotherton (Mary).
ROSEMARY FOR REMEMBRANCE. Fcap. 8vo. 3s. 6d. net.

Brown (Vincent)
MY BROTHER. Sq. 16mo. 2s. net.
ORDEAL BY COMPASSION. Crown 8vo. 6s. [*In preparation.*
TWO IN CAPTIVITY. Crown 8vo. 3s. 6d. [*In preparation.*

Buchan (John).
SCHOLAR GIPSIES. With 7 full-page Etchings by D. Y. CAMERON. Crown 8vo. 5s. net.
MUSA PISCATRIX. With 6 Etchings by E. PHILIP PIMLOTT. Crown 8vo. 5s. net.
GREY WEATHER. Crown 8vo. 5s. [*In preparation.*
JOHN BURNET OF BARNS. A Romance. Crown 8vo. 6s. [*In preparation.*

Campbell (Gerald).
THE JONESES AND THE ASTERISKS. A Story in Monologue. 6 Illustrations by F. H. TOWNSEND. Fcap. 8vo, 3s. 6d. net. [*Second Edition.*

Case (Robert H.).
ENGLISH EPITHALAMIES. Crown 8vo, 5s. net.

Castle (Mrs. Egerton).
MY LITTLE LADY ANNE. Sq. 16mo, 2s. net.

Chapman (Elizabeth Rachel)
MARRIAGE QUESTIONS IN MODERN FICTION. Crown 8vo, 3s. 6d. net.

Charles (Joseph F.).
THE DUKE OF LINDEN. Crown 8vo, 5s. [*In preparation.*

Cobb (Thomas).
CARPET COURTSHIP. Crown 8vo, 3s. 6d. [*In preparation.*
MR. PASSINGHAM. Crown 8vo, 3s. 6d. [*In preparation.*

Crane (Walter).
TOY BOOKS. Re-issue of.
THIS LITTLE PIG'S PICTURE BOOK, containing:
 I. THIS LITTLE PIG.
 II. THE FAIRY SHIP.
 III. KING LUCKIEBOY'S PARTY.
MOTHER HUBBARD'S PICTURE-BOOK, containing:
 IV. MOTHER HUBBARD.
 V. THE THREE BEARS.
 VI. THE ABSURD A. B. C.

Crane (Walter)—*continued.*
CINDERELLA'S PICTURE BOOK, containing:
 VII. CINDERELLA.
 VIII. PUSS IN BOOTS.
 IX. VALENTINE AND ORSON.
Each Picture-Book containing three Toy Books, complete with end papers and covers, together with collective titles, end-papers, decorative cloth cover, and newly written Preface by WALTER CRANE, 4s. 6d. The Nine Parts as above may be had separately at 1s. each.

Crackanthorpe (Hubert).
VIGNETTES. A Miniature Journal of Whim and Sentiment. Fcap. 8vo, boards. 2s. 6d. net.

Craig (R. Manifold).
THE SACRIFICE OF FOOLS. Crown 8vo, 6s.

Crosse (Victoria).
THE WOMAN WHO DIDN'T. Crown 8vo, 3s. 6d. net. [*Third Edition.*

Custance (Olive).
OPALS: Poems. Fcap. 8vo. 3s. 6d. net.

Croskey (Julian).
MAX. Crown 8vo. 6s.

Dalmon (C. W.).
SONG FAVOURS. Sq. 16mo. 3s. 6d. net.

D'Arcy (Ella).
MONOCHROMES. Crown 8vo. 3s. 6d. net.
POOR HUMAN NATURE. Crown 8vo. 3s. 6d. [*In preparation.*

Dawe (W. Carlton).
YELLOW AND WHITE. Crown 8vo. 3s. 6d. net.
KAKEMONOS. Crown 8vo. 3s. 6d. net.

Dawson (A. J.)
MERE SENTIMENT. Crown 8vo. 3s. 6d. net.
MIDDLE GREYNESS. Crown 8vo. 6s.

Davidson (John).
PLAYS: An Unhistorical Pastoral; A Romantic Farce; Bruce, a Chronicle Play; Smith, a Tragic Farce; Scaramouch in Naxos, a Pantomime. Small 4to. 7s. 6d. net.

Davidson (John)—*continued.*
 FLEET STREET ECLOGUES. Fcap. 8vo, buckram. 4s. 6d. net. [*Third Edition.*
 FLEET STREET ECLOGUES. 2nd Series. Fcap. 8vo, buckram. 4s. 6d. net. [*Second Edition.*
 A RANDOM ITINERARY. Fcap. 8vo, 5s. net.
 BALLADS AND SONGS. Fcap. 8vo, 5s. net. [*Fourth Edition.*
 NEW BALLADS. Fcap. 8vo, 4s. 6d. net. [*Second Edition.*

De Lyrienne (Richard).
 THE QUEST OF THE GILT-EDGED GIRL. Sq. 16mo. 1s. net.

De Tabley (Lord).
 POEMS, DRAMATIC AND LYRICAL. By JOHN LEICESTER WARREN (Lord de Tabley). Five Illustrations and Cover by C. S. RICKETTS. Crown 8vo. 7s. 6d. net. [*Third Edition.*
 POEMS, DRAMATIC AND LYRICAL. Second Series. Crown 8vo. 5s. net.

Devereux (Roy).
 THE ASCENT OF WOMAN. Crown 8vo. 3s. 6d. net.

Dick (Chas. Hill).
 ENGLISH SATIRES. Crown 8vo. 5s. net. [*In preparation.*

Dix (Gertrude).
 THE GIRL FROM THE FARM. Crown 8vo. 3s. 6d. net. [*Second Edition.*

Dostoievsky (F.).
 POOR FOLK. Translated from the Russian by LENA MILMAN. With a Preface by GEORGE MOORE. Crown 8vo. 3s. 6d net.

Dowie (Menie Muriel).
 SOME WHIMS OF FATE. Post 8vo. 2s. 6d. net.

Duer (Caroline, and Alice).
 POEMS. Fcap. 8vo. 3s. 6d. net.

Egerton (George)
 KEYNOTES. Crown 8vo. 3s. 6d. net. [*Eighth Edition.*
 DISCORDS. Crown 8vo 3s. 6d. net. [*Fifth Edition.*
 SYMPHONIES. Crown 8vo. 6s. [*Second Edition.*
 FANTASIAS. Crown 8vo. 3s. 6d.
 THE HAZARD OF THE HILL. Crown 8vo. 6s. [*In preparation.*

Eglinton (John).
 TWO ESSAYS ON THE REMNANT. Post 8vo, wrappers. 1s. 6d. net. [*Second Edition.*

Farr (Florence).
 THE DANCING FAUN. Crown 8vo. 3s. 6d. net.

Fea (Allan).
 THE FLIGHT OF THE KING: A full, true, and particular account of the escape of His Most Sacred Majesty King Charles II. after the Battle of Worcester, with Sixteen Portraits in Photogravure and over 100 other Illustrations. Demy 8vo. 21s. net.

Field (Eugene).
 THE LOVE AFFAIRS OF A BIBLIOMANIAC. Post 8vo. 3s. 6d. net.
 LULLABY LAND: Poems for Children. Edited, with Introduction, by KENNETH GRAHAME. With 200 Illustrations by CHAS. ROBINSON. Uncut or gilt edges. Crown 8vo. 6s.

Fifth (George).
 THE MARTYR'S BIBLE. Crown 8vo. 6s. [*In preparation.*

Fleming (George).
 FOR PLAIN WOMEN ONLY. Fcap. 8vo. 3s. 6d. net.

Flowerdew (Herbert).
 A CELIBATE'S WIFE. Crown 8vo. 6s. [*In preparation.*

Fletcher (J. S.).
 THE WONDERFUL WAPENTAKE. By "A SON OF THE SOIL." With 18 Full-page Illustrations by J. A. SYMINGTON. Crown 8vo. 5s. 6d. net.
 LIFE IN ARCADIA. With 20 Illustrations by PATTEN WILSON. Crown 8vo. 5s. net.
 GOD'S FAILURES. Crown 8vo. 3s. 6d. net.
 BALLADS OF REVOLT. Sq. 32mo. 2s. 6d. net.
 THE MAKING OF MATTHIAS. With 40 Illustrations and Decorations by LUCY KEMP-WELCH. Crown 8vo. 6s.

Ford, (James L.).
 THE LITERARY SHOP, AND OTHER TALES. Fcap. 8vo. 3s. 6d. net.

Frederic (Harold).
MARCH HARES. Crown 8vo. 3s. 6d. net. [*Third Edition.*
MRS. ALBERT GRUNDY: OBSERVATIONS IN PHILISTIA. Fcap. 8vo. 3s. 6d. net. [*Second Edition.*

Fuller (H. B.).
THE PUPPET BOOTH. Twelve Plays. Crown 8vo. 4s. 6d. net.

Gale (Norman).
ORCHARD SONGS. Fcap. 8vo. 5s. net.

Garnett (Richard).
POEMS. Crown 8vo. 5s. net.
DANTE, PETRARCH, CAMOENS, cxxiv Sonnets, rendered in English. Crown 8vo. 5s. net.

Geary (Sir Nevill).
A LAWYER'S WIFE. Crown 8vo. 6s. [*Second Edition.*

Gibson (Charles Dana).
DRAWINGS: Eighty-Five Large Cartoons. Oblong Folio. 20s.
PICTURES OF PEOPLE. Eighty-Five Large Cartoons. Oblong folio. 20s.
LONDON: AS SEEN BY C. D. GIBSON. Text and Illustrations. Large folio, 12 × 18 inches. 20s. [*In preparation.*
THE PEOPLE OF DICKENS. Six Large Photogravures. Proof Impressions from Plates, in a Portfolio. 20s.

Gilliat-Smith (E.)
THE HYMNS OF PRUDENTIUS. In the Rhythm of the Original. Pott 4to. 5s. net.

Gleig (Charles)
WHEN ALL MEN STARVE. Crown 8vo. 3s. 6d.
THE EDGE OF HONESTY. Crown 8vo. 6s. [*In preparation.*

Gosse (Edmund).
THE LETTERS OF THOMAS LOVELL BEDDOES. Now first edited. Pott 8vo. 5s. net.

Grahame (Kenneth).
PAGAN PAPERS. Fcap. 8vo. 5s. net. [*Out of Print at present.*
THE GOLDEN AGE. Crown 8vo. 3s. 6d. net. [*Seventh Edition.*
See EUGENE FIELD'S LULLABY LAND

Greene (G. A.).
ITALIAN LYRISTS OF TO-DAY. Translations in the original metres from about thirty-five living Italian poets, with bibliographical and biographical notes. Crown 8vo. 5s. net.

Greenwood (Frederick).
IMAGINATION IN DREAMS. Crown 8vo. 5s. net.

Grimshaw (Beatrice Ethel).
BROKEN AWAY. Crown 8vo. 3s. 6d. net.

Hake (T. Gordon).
A SELECTION FROM HIS POEMS. Edited by Mrs. MEYNELL. With a Portrait after D. G. ROSSETTI. Crown 8vo. 5s. net.

Hansson (Laura M.).
MODERN WOMEN. An English rendering of "DAS BUCH DER FRAUEN" by HERMIONE RAMSDEN. Subjects: Sonia Kovalevsky, George Egerton, Eleanora Duse, Amalie Skram, Marie Bashkirtseff, A. Ch. Edgren Leffler. Crown 8vo. 3s. 6d. net.

Hansson (Ola).
YOUNG OFEG'S DITTIES. A Translation from the Swedish. By GEORGE EGERTON. Crown 8vo. 3s. 6d. net.

Harland (Henry).
GREY ROSES. Crown 8vo, 3s. 6d. net.

Hay (Colonel John).
POEMS INCLUDING "THE PIKE COUNTY BALLADS" (Author's Edition), with Portrait of the Author. Crown 8vo. 4s. 6d. net.
CASTILIAN DAYS. Crown 8vo. 4s. 6d. net.
SPEECH AT THE UNVEILING OF THE BUST OF SIR WALTER SCOTT IN WESTMINSTER ABBEY. With a Drawing of the Bust. Sq. 16mo. 1s. net.

Hayes (Alfred).
THE VALE OF ARDEN AND OTHER POEMS. Fcap. 8vo. 3s. 6d. net.

Hazlitt (William).
LIBER AMORIS; OR, THE NEW PYGMALION. Edited, with an Introduction, by RICHARD LE GALLIENNE. To which is added an exact transcript of the original MS., Mrs. Hazlitt's Diary in Scotland, and letters never before published. Portrait after BEWICK, and facsimile letters. 400 Copies only. 4to, 364 pp., buckram. 21s. net.

Heinemann (William).
THE FIRST STEP; A Dramatic Moment. Small 4to. 3s. 6d. net.

Henniker (Florence).
IN SCARLET AND GREY. (With THE SPECTRE OF THE REAL by FLORENCE HENNIKER and THOMAS HARDY.) Crown 8vo. 3s. 6d. net. [*Second Edition.*

Hickson (Mrs. Murray).
SHADOWS OF LIFE. Post 8vo. 3s. 6d. [*In preparation.*

Hopper (Nora).
BALLADS IN PROSE. Sm. 4to. 6s.
UNDER QUICKEN BOUGHS. Crown 8vo. 5s. net.

Housman (Clemence).
THE WERE WOLF. With 6 Illustrations by LAURENCE HOUSMAN. Sq. 16mo. 3s. 6d. net.

Housman (Laurence).
GREEN ARRAS: Poems. With 6 Illustrations, Title-page, Cover Design, and End Papers by the Author. Crown 8vo. 5s. net.
GODS AND THEIR MAKERS. Crown 8vo, 3s. 6d. net.

Irving (Laurence).
GODEFROI AND YOLANDE: A Play. Sm. 4to. 3s. 6d. net.
[*In preparation.*

Jalland (G. H.)
THE SPORTING ADVENTURES OF MR. POPPLE. Coloured Plates. Oblong 4to, 14 × 10 inches. 6s.
[*In preparation.*

James (W. P.)
ROMANTIC PROFESSIONS: A Volume of Essays. Crown 8vo. 5s. net.

Johnson (Lionel).
THE ART OF THOMAS HARDY: Six Essays. With Etched Portrait by WM. STRANG, and Bibliography by JOHN LANE. Crown 8vo. 5s. 6d. net. [*Second Edition.*

Johnson (Pauline).
WHITE WAMPUM: Poems. Crown 8vo. 5s. net.

Johnstone (C. E.).
BALLADS OF BOY AND BEAK. Sq. 32mo. 2s. net.

Kemble (E. W.)
KEMBLE'S COONS. 30 Drawings of Coloured Children and Southern Scenes. Oblong 4to. 6s.

King (K. Douglas).
THE CHILD WHO WILL NEVER GROW OLD. Crown 8vo. 5s.

King (Maud Egerton).
ROUND ABOUT A BRIGHTON COACH OFFICE. With over 30 Illustrations by LUCY KEMP-WELCH. Crown 8vo. 5s. net.

Lander (Harry).
WEIGHED IN THE BALANCE. Crown 8vo. 6s.

The Lark.
BOOK THE FIRST. Containing Nos. 1 to 12. With numerous Illustrations by GELETT BURGESS and Others. Small 4to. 6s.
BOOK THE SECOND. Containing Nos. 13 to 24. With numerous Illustrations by GELETT BURGESS and Others. Small 4to. 6s.
[*All published.*

Leather (R. K.).
VERSES. 250 copies. Fcap. 8vo. 3s. net.

Lefroy (Edward Cracroft.)
POEMS. With a Memoir by W. A. GILL, and a reprint of Mr. J. A. SYMONDS' Critical Essay on "Echoes from Theocritus." Cr. 8vo. Photogravure Portrait. 5s. net.

Le Gallienne (Richard).
PROSE FANCIES. With Portrait of the Author by WILSON STEER. Crown 8vo. 5s. net.
[*Fourth Edition.*
THE BOOK BILLS OF NARCISSUS. An Account rendered by RICHARD LE GALLIENNE. With a Frontispiece. Crown 8vo. 3s. 6d. net.
[*Third Edition.*
ROBERT LOUIS STEVENSON, AN ELEGY, AND OTHER POEMS, MAINLY PERSONAL. Crown 8vo. 4s. 6d. net.

Le Gallienne (Richard)—
continued.
> ENGLISH POEMS. Crown 8vo. 4s. 6d. net.
> *[Fourth Edition, revised.*
> GEORGE MEREDITH: Some Characteristics. With a Bibliography (much enlarged) by JOHN LANE, portrait, &c. Crown 8vo. 5s. 6d. net. *[Fourth Edition.*
> THE RELIGION OF A LITERARY MAN. Crown 8vo. 3s. 6d. net.
> *[Fifth Thousand.*
> RETROSPECTIVE REVIEWS, A LITERARY LOG, 1891-1895. 2 vols. Crown 8vo. 9s. net.
> PROSE FANCIES. (Second Series). Crown 8vo. 5s. net.
> THE QUEST OF THE GOLDEN GIRL. Crown 8vo. 6s. *[Fifth Edition.*
> LOVE IN LONDON: Poems. Crown 8vo. 4s. 6d. net. *(In preparation.*
> See also HAZLITT, WALTON and COTTON.

Legge (A. E. J.).
> THREADBARE SOULS. Crown 8vo. 6s. *[In preparation.*

Linden (Annie).
> GOLD. A Dutch Indian story. Crown 8vo. 3s. 6d. net.

Lipsett (Caldwell).
> WHERE THE ATLANTIC MEETS THE LAND. Crown 8vo. 3s. 6d. net.

Locke (W. J.).
> DERELICTS. Crown 8vo. 6s.

Lowry (H. D.).
> MAKE BELIEVE. Illustrated by CHARLES ROBINSON. Crown 8vo, gilt edges or uncut. 6s.
> WOMEN'S TRAGEDIES. Crown 8vo. 3s. 6d. net.
> THE HAPPY EXILE. With 6 Etchings by E. PHILIP PIMLOTT. (Arcady Library, Vol. V.) Crown 8vo. 6s.

Lucas (Winifred).
> UNITS: Poems. Fcap. 8vo. 3s. 6d. net.

Lynch (Hannah).
> THE GREAT GALEOTO AND FOLLY OR SAINTLINESS. Two Plays, from the Spanish of JOSÉ ECHEGARAY, with an Introduction. Small 4to. 5s. 6d. net.

McChesney (Dora Greenwell).
> BEATRIX INFELIX. A Summer Tragedy in Rome. Crown 8vo. 3s. 6d. *[In preparation.*

Macgregor (Barrington).
> KING LONGBEARD. With nearly 100 Illustrations by CHARLES ROBINSON. Small 4to. 6s.

Machen (Arthur).
> THE GREAT GOD PAN AND THE INMOST LIGHT. Crown 8vo. 3s. 6d. net. *[Second Edition.*
> THE THREE IMPOSTORS. Crown 8vo. 3s. 6d. net.

Macleod (Fiona).
> THE MOUNTAIN LOVERS. Crown 8vo. 3s. 6d. net.

Makower (Stanley V.).
> THE MIRROR OF MUSIC. Crown 8vo. 3s. 6d. net.
> CECILIA. Crown 8vo. 5s.

Mangan (James Clarence).
> SELECTED POEMS. With a Biographical and Critical Preface by LOUISE IMOGEN GUINEY. Crown 8vo. 5s. net.

Mathew (Frank).
> THE WOOD OF THE BRAMBLES. Crown 8vo. 6s.
> A CHILD IN THE TEMPLE. Crown 8vo. 3s. 6d.
> THE SPANISH WINE. Crown 8vo. 3s. 6d. *[In preparation.*
> AT THE RISING OF THE MOON. Crown 8vo. 3s. 6d.

Marzials (Theo.).
> THE GALLERY OF PIGEONS AND OTHER POEMS. Post 8vo. 4s. 6d. net.

Meredith (George).
> THE FIRST PUBLISHED PORTRAIT OF THIS AUTHOR, engraved on the wood by W. BISCOMBE GARDNER, after the painting by G. F. WATTS. Proof copies on Japanese vellum, signed by painter and engraver. £1 1s. net.

Meynell (Mrs.).
> POEMS. Fcap. 8vo. 3s. 6d. net.
> *[Fifth Edition.*
> THE RHYTHM OF LIFE AND OTHER ESSAYS. Fcap. 8vo. 3s. 6d. net.
> *[Fifth Edition.*

Meynell (Mrs.)—*continued*.
  THE COLOUR OF LIFE AND OTHER ESSAYS. Fcap. 8vo. 3s. 6d. net. [*Fifth Edition.*
  THE CHILDREN. Fcap. 8vo. 3s. 6d. net. [*Second Edition.*

Miller (Joaquin).
  THE BUILDING OF THE CITY BEAUTIFUL. Fcap. 8vo. With a Decorated Cover. 5s. net.

Milman (Helen).
  IN THE GARDEN OF PEACE. With 24 Illustrations by EDMUND H. NEW. Crown 8vo. 5s. net.

Money-Coutts (F. B.).
  POEMS. Crown 8vo. 3s. 6d. net.

Monkhouse (Allan).
  BOOKS AND PLAYS: A Volume of Essays on Meredith, Borrow, Ibsen, and others. Crown 8vo. 5s. net.
  A DELIVERANCE. Crown 8vo. 5s. [*In preparation.*

Nesbit (E.).
  A POMANDER OF VERSE. Crown 8vo. 5s. net.
  IN HOMESPUN. Crown 8vo. 3s. 6d. net.

Nettleship (J. T.).
  ROBERT BROWNING: Essays and Thoughts. Portrait. Crown 8vo. 5s. 6d. net. [*Third Edition.*

Nicholson (Claud).
  UGLY IDOL. Crown 8vo. 3s. 6d. net.

Noble (Jas. Ashcroft).
  THE SONNET IN ENGLAND AND OTHER ESSAYS. Crown 8vo. 5s. net.

Oppenheim (M.).
  A HISTORY OF THE ADMINISTRATION OF THE ROYAL NAVY, and of Merchant Shipping in relation to the Navy from MDIX to MDCLX, with an introduction treating of the earlier period. With Illustrations. Demy 8vo. 15s. net.

Orred (Meta).
  GLAMOUR. Crown 8vo. 6s.

O'Shaughnessy (Arthur).
  HIS LIFE AND HIS WORK. With Selections from his Poems. By LOUISE CHANDLER MOULTON. Portrait and Cover Design. Fcap. 8vo. 5s. net.

Oxford Characters.
  A series of lithographed portraits by WILL ROTHENSTEIN, with text by F. YORK POWELL and others. 200 copies only, folio. £3 3s. net.

Pennell (Elizabeth Robins).
  THE FEASTS OF AUTOLYCUS: THE DIARY OF A GREEDY WOMAN. Fcap. 8vo. 3s. 6d. net.

Peters (Wm. Theodore).
  POSIES OUT OF RINGS. Sq. 16mo. 2s. 6d. net.

Phillips (Stephen)
  THE WOMAN WITH A DEAD SOUL, AND OTHER POEMS. Crown 8vo. 4s. 6d. net.

Plarr (Victor).
  IN THE DORIAN MOOD: Poems. Crown 8vo. 5s. net.

Posters in Miniature: over 250 reproductions of French, English and American Posters with Introduction by EDWARD PENFIELD. Large crown 8vo. 5s. net.

Price (A. T. G.).
  SIMPLICITY. Sq. 16mo. 2s. net.

Radford (Dollie).
  SONGS AND OTHER VERSES. Fcap. 8vo. 4s. 6d. net.

Risley (R. V.).
  THE SENTIMENTAL VIKINGS. Post 8vo. 2s. 6d. net.

Rhys (Ernest).
  A LONDON ROSE AND OTHER RHYMES. Crown 8vo. 5s. net

Robertson (John M.).
  NEW ESSAYS TOWARDS A CRITICAL METHOD. Crown 8vo. 6s. net.

St. Cyres (Lord).
THE LITTLE FLOWERS OF ST. FRANCIS: A new rendering into English of the Fioretti di San Francesco. Crown 8vo. 5s. net. [*In preparation.*

Seaman (Owen).
THE BATTLE OF THE BAYS. Fcap. 8vo. 3s. 6d. net. [*Third Edition.*
HORACE AT CAMBRIDGE. Crown 8vo. 3s. 6d. net.

Sedgwick (Jane Minot).
SONGS FROM THE GREEK. Fcap. 8vo. 3s. 6d. net.

Setoun (Gabriel).
THE CHILD WORLD: Poems. With over 200 Illustrations by CHARLES ROBINSON. Crown 8vo, gilt edges or uncut. 6s.

Sharp (Evelyn).
WYMPS: Fairy Tales. With Coloured Illustrations by Mrs. PERCY DEARMER. Small 4to, decorated cover. 6s.
AT THE RELTON ARMS. Crown 8vo. 3s. 6d. net.
THE MAKING OF A PRIG. Crown 8vo. 6s.
ALL THE WAY TO FAIRY LAND. With Coloured Illustrations by Mrs. PERCY DEARMER. Small 4to, decorated cover. 6s.

Shiel (M. P.).
PRINCE ZALESKI. Crown 8vo. 3s. 6d. net.
SHAPES IN THE FIRE. Crown 8vo. 3s. 6d. net.

Shore (Louisa).
POEMS. With an appreciation by FREDERIC HARRISON and a Portrait. Fcap. 8vo. 5s. net.

Shorter (Mrs. Clement) (Dora Sigerson).
THE FAIRY CHANGELING, AND OTHER POEMS. Crown 8vo. 3s. 6d. net.

Smith (John).
PLATONIC AFFECTIONS. Crown 8vo. 3s. 6d. net.

Stacpoole (H. de Vere).
PIERROT. Sq. 16mo. 2s. net.
DEATH, THE KNIGHT, AND THE LADY. Crown 8vo. 3s. 6d.

Stevenson (Robert Louis).
PRINCE OTTO. A Rendering in French by EGERTON CASTLE. Crown 8vo. 7s. 6d. net.
A CHILD'S GARDEN OF VERSES. With over 150 Illustrations by CHARLES ROBINSON. Crown 8vo. 5s. net. [*Third Edition.*

Stimson (F. J.)
KING NOANETT. A Romance of Devonshire Settlers in New England. With 12 Illustrations by HENRY SANDHAM. Crown 8vo. 6s.

Stoddart (Thos. Tod).
THE DEATH WAKE. With an Introduction by ANDREW LANG. Fcap. 8vo. 5s. net.

Street (G. S.).
EPISODES. Post 8vo. 3s. net.
MINIATURES AND MOODS. Fcap. 8vo. 3s. net.
QUALES EGO: A FEW REMARKS, IN PARTICULAR AND AT LARGE. Fcap. 8vo. 3s. 6d. net.
THE AUTOBIOGRAPHY OF A BOY. Fcap. 8vo. 3s. 6d. net.
THE WISE AND THE WAYWARD. Crown 8vo. 6s.

Sudermann (H.).
THE SINS OF THE FATHERS. A Translation of DER KATZENSTEG. By BEATRICE MARSHALL. Crown 8vo. 6s. [*In preparation.*

Swettenham (Sir F. A.)
MALAY SKETCHES. Crown 8vo. 5s. net. [*Second Edition.*

Syrett (Netta).
NOBODY'S FAULT. Crown 8vo. 3s. 6d. net. [*Second Edition.*
THE TREE OF LIFE. Crown 8vo. 6s.

Tabb (John B.).
POEMS. Sq. 32mo. 4s. 6d. net.
LYRICS. Sq. 32mo. 4s. 6d. net.

Taylor (Una).
NETS FOR THE WIND. Crown 8vo, 3s. 6d. net.

Tennyson (Frederick).
POEMS OF THE DAY AND YEAR. Crown 8vo. 5s. net.

Thimm (Carl A.).

A COMPLETE BIBLIOGRAPHY OF FENCING AND DUELLING, AS PRACTISED BY ALL EUROPEAN NATIONS FROM THE MIDDLE AGES TO THE PRESENT DAY. With a Classified Index, arranged Chronologically according to Languages. Illustrated with numerous Portraits of Ancient and Modern Masters of the Art. Title-pages and Frontispieces of some of the earliest works. Portrait of the Author by WILSON STEER. 4to. 21s. net.

Thompson (Francis)

POEMS. With Frontispiece by LAURENCE HOUSMAN. Pott 4to. 5s. net. [*Fourth Edition.*

SISTER-SONGS: An Offering to Two Sisters. With Frontispiece by LAURENCE HOUSMAN. Pott 4to. 5s. net.

Thoreau (Henry David).

POEMS OF NATURE. Selected and edited by HENRY S. SALT and FRANK B. SANBORN. Fcap. 8vo. 4s. 6d. net.

Traill (H. D.).

THE BARBAROUS BRITISHERS: A Tip-top Novel. Crown 8vo, wrapper. 1s. net.

FROM CAIRO TO THE SOUDAN FRONTIER. Crown 8vo. 5s. net.

Tynan Hinkson (Katharine).

CUCKOO SONGS. Fcap. 8vo. 5s. net.

MIRACLE PLAYS. OUR LORD'S COMING AND CHILDHOOD. With 6 Illustrations by PATTEN WILSON. Fcap. 8vo. 4s. 6d. net.

Wells (H. G.)

SELECT CONVERSATIONS WITH AN UNCLE, NOW EXTINCT. Fcap. 8vo. 3s. 6d. net.

Walton and Cotton.

THE COMPLEAT ANGLER. Edited by RICHARD LE GALLIENNE. With over 250 Illustrations by EDMUND H. NEW. Fcap. 4to, decorated cover. 15s. net.

Also to be had in thirteen 1s. parts.

Warden (Gertrude).

THE SENTIMENTAL SEX. Crown 8vo. 3s. 6d. net.

Watson (H. B. Marriott).

AT THE FIRST CORNER AND OTHER STORIES. Crown 8vo. 3s. 6d. net.

GALLOPING DICK. Crown 8vo. 6s.

THE HEART OF MIRANDA. Crown 8vo. 5s.

Watson (Rosamund Marriott).

VESPERTILIA AND OTHER POEMS. Fcap 8vo. 4s. 6d. net.

A SUMMER NIGHT AND OTHER POEMS. New Edition. Fcap. 8vo. 3s. net.

Watson (William).

THE FATHER OF THE FOREST AND OTHER POEMS. With New Photogravure Portrait of the Author. Fcap. 8vo. 3s. 6d. net. [*Fifth Edition.*

ODES AND OTHER POEMS. Fcap. 8vo. 4s. 6d. net. [*Fourth Edition.*

THE ELOPING ANGELS: A Caprice. Square 16mo. 3s. 6d. net. [*Second Edition.*

EXCURSIONS IN CRITICISM: being some Prose Recreations of a Rhymer. Crown 8vo. 5s. net. [*Second Edition.*

THE PRINCE'S QUEST AND OTHER POEMS. Fcap. 8vo. 4s. 6d. net. [*Third Edition.*

THE PURPLE EAST: A Series of Sonnets on England's Desertion of Armenia. With a Frontispiece after G. F. WATTS, R.A. Fcap. 8vo, wrappers. 1s. net. [*Third Edition.*

Watson (William)—*cont.*
  THE YEAR OF SHAME. With an Introduction by the BISHOP OF HEREFORD. Fcap. 8vo. 2s. 6d. net. [*Second Edition.*
  POEMS. A New Volume. Ready for Christmas. Fcap. 8vo. 4s. 6d. net.
  A Large Paper Edition at 12s. 6d. net.

Watt (Francis).
  THE LAW'S LUMBER ROOM. Fcap. 8vo. 3s. 6d. net. [*Second Edition.*
  FATHER ANTIC, THE LAW. Crown 8vo. 5s. net. [*In preparation.*

Watts-Dunton (Theodore).
  JUBILEE GREETING AT SPITHEAD TO THE MEN OF GREATER BRITAIN. Crown 8vo. 1s. net.
  THE COMING OF LOVE AND OTHER POEMS. Crown 8vo. 5s. net.

Wenzell (A. B.)
  IN VANITY FAIR. 70 Drawings. Oblong folio. 20s.

Wharton (H. T.)
  SAPPHO. Memoir, Text, Selected Renderings, and a Literal Translation by HENRY THORNTON WHARTON. With 3 Illustrations in Photogravure, and a Cover designed by AUBREY BEARDSLEY. With a Memoir of Mr. Wharton. Fcap. 8vo. 6s. net. [*Fourth Edition.*

Wotton (Mabel E.).
  DAY BOOKS. Crown 8vo. 3s. 6d. net.

Xenopoulos (Gregory).
  THE STEPMOTHER: A TALE OF MODERN ATHENS. Translated by MRS. EDMONDS. Crown 8vo. 2s. 6d. net.

THE YELLOW BOOK

An Illustrated Quarterly.

Pott 4to. 5s. net.

I. April 1894, 272 pp., 15 Illustrations. [*Out of print.*
II. July 1894, 364 pp., 23 Illustrations.
III. October 1894, 280 pp., 15 Illustrations.
IV. January 1895, 285 pp., 16 Illustrations.
V. April 1895, 317 pp., 14 Illustrations.
VI. July 1895, 335 pp., 16 Illustrations.
VII. October 1895, 320 pp., 20 Illustrations.
VIII. January 1896, 406 pp., 26 Illustrations.
IX. April 1896, 256 pp., 17 Illustrations.
X. July 1896, 340 pp., 13 Illustrations.
XI. October 1896, 342 pp., 12 Illustrations.
XII. January 1897, 350 pp., 14 Illustrations.
XIII. April 1897, 316 pp, 18 Illustrations.

BALLANTYNE PRESS

www.ingramcontent.com/pod-product-compliance
Ingram Content Group UK Ltd.
Pitfield, Milton Keynes, MK11 3LW, UK
UKHW051328180126
10157UKWH00026B/404